Introduction

This book describes the system I have been using successfully with kids for many years. It is written for parents with kids from toddlers to teenagers who have ever wondered why their child should turn to them rather than to drugs and suicide. It is a record and a guide for these parents to a program that is working successfully in the home and classroom to change these hostilities among our kids. To produce the necessary initiative in the classroom and in the home, I show kids how they can get what they want and be who they want to be by adopting an industry-based standard of achievement. Kids learn how to take responsibility for their actions. I will discuss quite candidly why our educational system is not able to offer the same success as an alternative and why all too often some parents realize too late the mistakes they make in bringing up their children.

How did I develop The System? Well, it happened almost by accident.

In 1980, I was fresh out of a university graduate program in behavioral science-three graduate years training cats to respond to commands by teaching them to ring a bell when they were hungry. Two years later I was completing an internship by helping to develop programs to change the unacceptable behavior of junior high school students using the same techniques I had learned with the cats. Unless their behaviors changed, the local school district would have to place these children outside the regular public school system. The programs were just as effective as the programs with the cats, and the children were admitted back into the public school system, where their problems started.

While I was pleased that the behavior modification programs worked, I was distressed because the systems I was experiencing and observing in the school and home weren't working. The systems themselves were creating a need to have "corrective" behavior programs, instead of simply functioning to educate children to be happy, successful people. Teachers and parents were nagging children ninety percent of the time and teaching and enjoying them ten percent of the time. It was a constant emotional turmoil. If we weren't able to raise our kids for success, then what were we doing? Whatever it was, it wasn't any fun.

During the early years of my teaching career I began to dabble in business or should I say with business ideas. "Others have money, I have ideas," I would proclaim like a self appointed candidate. The truth of the matter was, I was broke. Why should anyone in business listen to a penniless teacher? The thought never even crossed my mind. The attitude I CAN'T didn't exist. Whatever the mind can conceive, it can have. The idea of putting a man on the moon was given life long before the first microchip was developed-now we float in space. I'm an I CAN person with dreams. What does a broke, persistent dreamer do? He sells dreams.

I would call investors and tell them about a swell condo complex we could pick up for a pittance. It's always a pittance when the money belongs to the other guy. Some would react as if I were selling property on the moon. Finally, one of the investors, Mr. Mills, said that he wasn't interested in condos, but would be interested in making money. He lived in Bel-Air, California. At the time I was living in northwest Washington.

I could barely afford the rent for a three room flat, but I scraped together enough money for a round trip flight to Los Angeles. I can still remember sitting by his pool. For the first time in years I didn't do the talking. I sat and listened, waiting for the big deal.

He was thirty years older than I and had gone from rags to riches three times. Mr. Mills had some ideas about long-range success. He said, "Use things, love people and don't screw it up. Things don't have worth, only people do. A person can own all the real estate and jewels in the world and if they have no friends, their possessions will have no real worth. The wrong attitude doesn't work. Oh, it may pay for a little while, but in the end, you will lose. "He paused, sipped his drink and continued. "Remember, I'm talking long-range success. Why don't more people succeed? I'll tell you. Anybody can achieve if they operate the way life is supposed to operate. They must follow the laws of success. Most people just don't know how. They live in abject mediocrity physically, emotionally and intellectually. Change what they're thinking and you'll change how they live. Help others where they want to go and you'll live any lifestyle you choose. Attitude determines how an individual will live and what he will be-at any age."

We started a partnership developing network marketing that continues to this day. Mr. Mills turned my life around.

As I worked with Mr. Mills, I was surprised to discover that ninety percent of the people we worked with had an I CAN'T attitude while ten percent had an I CAN attitude. But as their attitude changed, so did their situation. I watched Mr. Mills telling people that they could do it. The scene was always the same. It reminded me of a little kid learning how to walk. Every time the kids fell down, Mr. Mills was there to encourage and reward their efforts. The kids always stood up again and took another step forward. When they did the work they got the pay, and those who got the pay did the work. It was a rewarding cycle of attitude and reward anchored in the work ethic.

If children are destined to live their adult years in Mr. Mills' world of business - they will leave home and school someday- then the systems I'd experienced and observed in the school and homes were artificial. We can best prepare our kids for success by finding systems that work, all the time. Not artificial systems that may only pay for a little while, but universal systems that children can use successfully throughout their entire lives.

Attitude and step-by-step management worked in business. Follow the steps and you win; fail and you lose.   It was a concrete system.

Developing a business attitude in a behavior management system became clearer. The principles of learning in the home and in the school needed to follow the same principles that exist in business. After all, that's where the child is destined. Our job as parents and teachers is to ensure that our children will be able to live their lives successfully in the real world after we parents and teachers have said our farewells. If they can't, then we've failed and all the excuses won't change it.

Before moving to Los Angeles, I returned to the state of Washington to complete a nine-month teaching contract. One weekend a month I commuted to Los Angeles to continue working with Mr. Mills. My colleagues at school would inquire how I could perform two professions, both teaching and business, but they weren't that different. Both professions worked with people from all different walks of life, helped them to see themselves in a different light and move forward. Whether I was teaching adults how to develop a better lifestyle or teaching children how to get a better education, it was the same. Their attitude and the reward management system made the difference. But my colleagues didn't understand, and this was reflected in their results with the children.

Schools differ only in shape. Kids are the same everywhere, and unfortunately so are most teachers and parents- ninety percent nagging and ten percent instruction. In this district the administration didn't handle any discipline problems, but threw them back to the teachers and parents like throwing runt fish back into the sea, without defining the size of a runt Teachers were perplexed and parents were in constant turmoil concerning the frequent phone calls from school about their children's lack of discipline. Each blamed the other for the problem, but nobody did anything about it.

The state of affairs was almost comical. During a fire drill students would jump out windows, climb flagpoles and play hide and seek with the teachers during rescue roll call. The benefits of two hours of instruction evaporated. When teachers would leave the room, students would run down the halls knocking on doors of other classrooms or lock the door so the teacher could not reenter.

"Bolt the windows and lock the doors when you leave the classroom," was Administration's reply. Sounds like a prison movie. And when they gave the solution, every one agreed like it was absolutely sane. Other disciplinary action consisted of screaming, yelling and interrogation.

I shared some ideas that I had been working with, but parents, teachers and administrators weren't too concerned about how business building principles applied to the classroom: Those who do the work get the pay, and those who get the pay do the work.

"What the hell does that have to do with education?" they asked. If they didn't care, I didn't care. I wasn't on a crusade.

I wasn't going to solve the school district's problem, but I was going to solve my own. I was hired to teach, not to yell ninety percent of the time. The use of business building principles appeared to frighten the school district and parents, so I decided to call it "The System."

I started to apply The System because the smoother a system operated, the more time I had to pursue students' needs and my own life. Sound selfish? Not really, just strikingly honest. Those who do the work get the pay. My pay for my commitment was a paycheck, time and peace of mind. Hard work alone will not attain success. To be successful takes more than work. It takes an inner edge of knowing what to do, why you are doing it, and having, as Mr. Mills said, the right attitude. Mr. Mills always said, "Success breeds success. Teach others to take responsibility for their actions and they will be rewarded for it. Help others where they want to go and you can live any lifestyle you desire."

Teachers and parents can never be rewarded unless the child is also rewarded. It's a win-win situation, just like in business. The more responsibility a child takes for his actions, the more learning and cooperation will develop. It's a winning cycle. But nobody at this school acted as if they knew this. The teachers, students, administrators and parents were not being responsible for their actions. Each was blaming the other. We needed responsibility all the way around. My first job was to convince the superintendent that I should have complete freedom with my program. I briefly described The System I was developing. I told him that I wanted to work directly with the parents on consequences for the students' actions. He laughed and said, "We teach here, not run a prison." I think he used the word bribery twice. I wanted to ask why paychecks were received and why he considered ninety percent nagging teaching. But confrontation was not the goal. The students needed an education and I needed sanity.

I requested that he give me three weeks and the students would be working ninety five percent of the time. No more behavior problems. The System worked beautifully and both the kids and I benefited.

At the end of three weeks, the superintendent gave me full authority with one stipulation: They wanted me to handle off campus problems. Parents had been complaining about their children arriving home late from school and receiving notices from other teachers of their children's disrespect to adults around campus.

I called the concerned parents and explained the success principle: Those who do the work get the pay, and those who get the pay always do the work. The idea made sense. They also knew how successfully The System had been working at the school, and they agreed to use it in their homes. One parent said, "Sounds fair to me. What's the fuss?"

In two months, the program had thirty percent more students. The students and parents had time and peace of mind. Other teachers began seeking the gold, but the new program involved change. Change? That meant work. "We don't have the time" they said. I told them we never have time; we make time. But they didn't care, so neither did I. They spent ninety percent of their time fretting, worrying and nagging. Ten percent of their time was spent actively teaching. They had their own responsibility. They, like the students, wanted someone to fret and worry about their situation. When school was out, I left for Los Angeles. I knew The System had reached a dynamic development, but I had to do some field-testing to prove its worth. So every day for six months I sat in a different classroom with different teachers, students and management systems.

One day I was working in a lower middle-income school. The school looked as if it should have been condemned, but students were burgeoning beyond capacity. It was not my first day, and the results of The System had been recognized.

As I was beginning to drive away from the school site, the principal approached me from the opposite side of the street. He described a special discipline program for children that needed full time supervision. I really didn't want to work in just one place, but the offer was made worth my time. As Mr. Mills would have said, "Business is business. Trade every second for value."   So I traded.

The next day I arrived to observe the present program. As I approached the large auditorium I was smacked by a din of noise.   When the door opened I could hardly believe the sight. Thirty children were running loose, swinging from the stage curtains and jumping on the piano. In pursuit were five adults yelling, '"No, no, no, no..."

Just like in Oregon, I told the principal that I wanted to work directly with the parents on consequences for the students' actions. Other teachers could not influence the program. Within these guidelines I promised to have only eight students on detention in thirty days. I was eliminating my own job.

The System was an absolute success. Yet one social worker took me into private conference to describe the very special and delicate needs of one child, who, according to the consequences of The System had opted by her actions to spend time after school. The social worker insisted that this child had special needs beyond the program.

"The child's home environment will not tolerate additional time. Of course, you can see this child's special needs? Therefore, I'll just take this child with me," she said.

I showed the social worker the child was aware of the consequences; that the child, through her actions, had actually volunteered to spend the additional time. The child was testing the program, like people test the laws of a new nation.

"The child knows more than she'd like us to think," I said.   While we were talking the child was screaming, cursing and spitting on the floor.

The social worker insisted, "The child will come with me!" I suggested she take the matter up with the school principal.

She headed for the front office with a smirk on her face. Ten minutes later she returned to the door and yelled, "I hold you responsible for what happens here!"

The child completed the program. A few days later she brought in some cookies for the principal and me. Responsibility is a learned behavior with learned rewards.

Raising kids for success not only creates a better future for our kids, but also creates happiness now for parents, teachers and children.

1

Born to Win-Conditioned to Lose

Raising kids for success is every parents dream, but most just don't know what to do.

I've been working for the public school system as a special educator for eight years, helping kids acquire the skill and attitudes necessary to insure their success as kids and ultimately as adults. I work with kids and teachers in the classroom, and with kids and parents -in their homes.

Over the years, I've developed The System, a very successful program that helps kids learn to get what they want through being responsible for their actions.

I've been using The System with my own son Michael since he was 21 days old.   His mother complained that he was refusing to nurse, and Mom didn't know what to do. I suggested she change him and then put him down in his crib for 20 minutes with no further fuss.   A tear glistened in her eye.

"Michael will be all right," I said. "He won't starve.   Do you want this behavior all the time?"

She changed him, put him down in his crib, and closed the door. Michael cried and screamed. After 20 minutes she picked him up and offered him her breast. Michael had no reservations. He drank voraciously. Whining and playing with his food during mealtime has never occurred again to this day.

Michael's needs may have been basic, but he learned an important law of success: How to change his behavior to get what he wants. Will show you how to create the changes you want to see in your own kids. They can achieve the success in life that is the possible future for every child.

To acquire their needs through responsible action is the basic lesson you will be teaching your child. Their childish attitude of whining and demanding to get their needs gradually fades, while they increasingly learn that they really are in control of what they get. They learn how to get what they want in the home and in the classroom by following the same expectations and codes of behavior that will be expected of them as adults. They will learn how to use the same attitudes that we as adults use to get our rewards. That's the beauty of the program-they learn the skills of success that most adults have had to learn through the school of "hard knocks." These responsible children grow-up to be very successful adults who never lose their childlike nature because they have what they want, and they know how to get what they don't have.

You'll teach them that life isn't complicated; it's really just a game. And when children learn the rules, they'll achieve better, farther, faster and easier. Ever try to play a game without knowing the rules? It's stressful and frustrating, but that's just what kids have been asked to do. Have you ever started a new job and didn't know all the playing rules? Did you feel like you were on stage with the wrong script? It's uncomfortable and not a lot of fun. Unless they know the rules, kids won't even have fun being kids when they're kids, let alone having fun when they're adults.

Did I make up the rules? No. They were here when I arrived, and they were here when you arrived. The only thing we're doing now is teaching the rules to the kids. If they learn now that achievement is fun, when they get out of school they'll be one super group of kids reaching beyond their own limits.

Have you ever said to yourself, "Boy, if only I had known that a few years ago." Our kids will have already learned how the system works because their learning hasn't been by accident.   It has been on purpose.

#1. KIDS IN THE GAME OF LIFE

We are all born with the capacity for greatness and success. Success isn't just acquiring wealth, yet one who is financially independent in our society is generally happier than one who is poor and without dignity. It also is obvious to see that those who use their talents for their own benefit are far more content than those who criticize and envy the progress of others. Success really is the same for everybody. WHAT EVERYBODY WANTS IS TO HAVE WHAT THEY WANT. Successful people know how to get from where they are to where they want to go. Raising kids for success is teaching them how to do this. If our kids accomplish this, they can achieve almost anything they desire.

At birth we all are pointed in the right direction for success because we are all born with the basic ability to play the game. Isn't that simply fantastic! Think about this. ALL CHILDREN ARE BORN TO WIN. Kids already know how to get what they want, but what a baby wants to win is very basic. Children's needs are simple. How do they feel about a particular situation? Cold is bad. Warm is good. Pain is awful. Hunger is terrible. They are born with the ability to get to their destination, which is to survive. They haven't learned the behaviors; they just know how to acquire their needs.   A loud, healthy cry will usually do the trick to get Mom and Dad to respond.

But the game of life never really changes. They'll still need hugs, toys, and dry pants, but it will take more than a whine for another person besides their parents to cooperate. And without the cooperation of other people, kids will never be successful. Good business people know that business is people. Things have no value, only people do. People who work with things have fewer options. People who work with people usually write their own ticket. If kids are going to be successful, they have to learn how to work with other people. Without the cooperation of others, kids can acquire the basics, but there's more to the game of life than just food and shelter. Raise kids for complete success.

Kids can achieve to almost any level they desire, especially in our time in history. The opportunities are exciting. We have the highest standard of living the world has ever seen. For the first time in the history of mankind we don't have to work twelve hours a day just to put food on the table; in fact, we have twice as much leisure time as we do working time. We have mobility, health, the longest life spans, and every opportunity to achieve to any level or direction of success we choose. The possibilities are endless. Why is it then that so often so many children barely reach beyond the basics of not even knowing how to achieve their daily needs, let alone how to be happy? Why are some people successful and others not?

These questions haunt parents and teachers today and yet, for thousands of years, all over the world, parents have been raising millions of happy, decent children. The mere fact mat we've come as far as we have out of the caves and into the skyscrapers is an indication that the process has been successful. But for some reason, recently people seem to have lost their direction and the ability to play the game of life successfully. Acquiring the ability to play the game isn't as clear perhaps as it has been in the past. Raising kids in the past could very well have been easier, and not because the lifestyle was simpler. People do long for the good old days but most couldn't survive because they couldn't get along without Kleenex or air conditioning. The past was not simpler, but different: around 1900, over ninety percent of the population lived on farms, now over ninety percent live in the cities.

The modern city dweller has almost forgotten his dependence on agricultural cycles. We give most of our attention to irregular business cycles, which affect our scale of living much more than the cycles of the seasons, which govern agriculture.

Being closer to an agrarian lifestyle teaches us more directly the way life is supposed to operate. There is little room for debate on the farm about how life works. If you plant you will reap - if you don't plant you won't reap. This isn't an option for the farmer, its a law of success. Just because we move from the country to the city doesn't change the law. Laws do not change. There are certain laws that all children and adults must obey, in order to be successful at the game of life.

Human life is governed by certain predictable laws. Whether you are aware of their existence or not is irrelevant. Not all of us are aware of nature's physical laws, like the law of gravity, but they exist and their existence affects us-every one of us-every day of our lives. Most of us have heard of the physical laws governing our world, but few of us have become familiar with the laws, which more closely affect our personal lives; that determine the absolute direction and destination in the game of life. There are many laws, but they are all minor parts of one major law that governs success: The law of cause and effect.

Everything in the universe operates on the law of cause and effect. There are no exceptions to this. Nothing does or will happen by accident. For every effect mere is a cause. You have only to take care of the cause and the effect will, without exception, take care of itself. Good cause, good effect. No cause, no effect. Bad cause, bad effect. It's good to be a student of cause, because there is a reason for everything that happens. If you don't like the effect, you change the cause.   Anything that's occurring in your life, whether it's happening to you personally or whether you see it in the behaviors and the actions of the people you encounter, you have created, intentionally or unintentionally. That is a fact. It is a law of the universe. Nothing you can think about or whine about will change the law.

You may kid yourselves at one time or another by saying a particular action didn't count. But it all counts. There are no practice games and there are no scrimmages. Every day, every second of your life is a Super Bowl. It's played to win and in the game of life there are no timeouts. You can't stop the clock or turn it back. EVERYTHING CHANGES IN RESPONSE TO YOUR CAUSE. Nothing stays the same. What kind of life you and your children choose to lead-rich or poor, happy or sad-depends on how well you to learn to play the game.

How you feel about your life doesn't change how things are, but what actions you take can affect their direction. Your actions become your assets or your liabilities.

How do you know when you're acting as an asset? Often parents are too close to the situation, to their kids, to really see that they're moving toward major problems. Frustration and headaches begin too casually. Situations change so gradually that you don't even know you're not having fun. You begin to think that raising your kids is supposed to be frustrating. Some days are good days, and some days are interspersed with worry, frustration, doubt and laughter. But if you're hearing more whines than smiles, then you need to change. It will not get better, only worse.

MAJOR PROBLEMS HAVE MINOR BEGINNINGS. Their growth is like a cancer, gradually growing until one day you have a major problem and you don't know what to do about it or how you even got there.

But there are telltale signs:

•Do you have moody children around the house?

•You don't look forward to seeing your kids every day?

•Do you feel you need a break from the kids?

•Is "No!" becoming an important word in your vocabulary around the house?

•Do you spend more time disciplining your kids rather than enjoying their company?

•Do your kids' behavior get on your nerves, daily?

•Do you find yourself nagging more than laughing?

•Do you find yourself saying "I guess it's OK. They'll probably grow out of it."

•Is the school telling you your child is just going through a phase?

•Do you find yourself thinking of fantasy dream vacations that don't include your kids?

•Do you wonder what to do when you see them doing something annoying or inappropriate?

•Are the kids in your life beginning to demand things rather than earn them?

•Are you dining and whining more than you're wining and dining lately?

•Are you using words like "hyperactive" at home or school to justify annoying behaviors?

If you answered "yes" to any of the questions, you may want to change the situations. The game of life is supposed to be fun, exciting to wake up to every morning. If its not, then you can change it by learning how to make your actions assets. It's a lot more fun.

Remember, THE LAW OF CAUSE AND EFFECT WILL DETERMINE YOUR KIDS' DIRECTION AND DESTINATION IN LIFE. Our destination is determined by direction. Our direction is determined by how we feel about our present situation and what actions we choose to take to change it.

How do you feel about the direction you and your kids are going? If you like your present situation, then don't change a thing. Close this book. But if you feel there is room for improvement, then take control.

To become successful in the game of life, kids must have the desire to reach beyond the basics. They must learn how to take personal responsibility for their actions. You've all met children and even adults who never learned how to be responsible. Whatever happens they blame others. They've never acquired the skills for success by learning how to achieve in the game of life beyond the basics. To acquire their needs they still whine, cry, pout, and even threaten. Some never learn, but your children can.

The System itself is simple to apply, but in order to understand how and why it works, let's first take a look at the laws of behavior, the laws of success, and how kids change.

2

The Laws of Behavior

The way kids act and the way kids learn is not due to chance, it is the result of four basic laws.

#1. EVERYBODY WANTS A LITTLE LOVE

Babies cry for it and men die for it. The need to be recognized is a powerful life force. All human beings crave recognition and every day they change their behavior to achieve it. How children acquire recognition doesn't happen spontaneously, it is learned.

Whether the recognition is received as punishment or affection makes little difference to children as long as they get it. That's how strong it is. Often, we as parents teach our children to respond with unacceptable behavior by being inconsistent with the use of rewards and punishments. For example, during the bedtime ritual, Tommy whines and nags his parents. Depending on the mood of the parents, sometimes Tommy gets cuddled and sometimes he gets punished.

What is mom teaching Tommy? How to be a neurotic. Imagine yourself going to work not knowing if you'll be paid, slapped or fired. Imagine your boss' rewards and responses going on and off like a glove, totally unrelated to your work and actions. You'd soon have an ulcer and a nervous twitch. Now imagine yourself in a work situation like this in which you can't quit, but must endure. Tommy can't quit. He can't find a new home with different parents. He must learn how to survive and get his recognition. Sometimes he'll get cuddled and sometimes he'll get punished depending on the mood of his parents, but he will be recognized.

Our children are only doing what they've been taught to do and they do it quite well. With clearly defined behaviors and consistent consequences, children can learn how to be recognized through responsible actions instead of bad behavior. And they will learn, because everybody wants a little love.

#2. REWARD A BEHAVIOR AND YOU'LL GET THAT BEHAVIOR

Rewards are privileges. As an adult, it's expected that all privileges must be earned. Parents, and even teachers, receive money for their labors. Money isn't the real goal, however, you really work for the privileges money can buy. The privileges of flicking on a switch for light and turning a dial for temperature, the simple privilege of enjoying a hamburger and fries without actually having to butcher a cow or dig a potato. Whatever the privilege, It is naturally tied to some action. The more productive action and less bratty behavior, the higher the salary and the more privileges you receive. The less productive the action and brattier the behavior, the fewer privileges.

Reward for labor must be clearly defined and consistent. Those who get the pay do the work; those who don't get the pay don't do the work. How long would you labor without reward?

What does all this have to do with children? Children and adults obey the rules for the same reasons they break them. Fail to pay an adult for just labor and punish for no probable cause and I'll introduce you to a real crank. Do the same to a child and I'll show you one bratty kid. What makes people conform? Benefits for the right actions, clearly given.

I remember when I first met Tommy. That kid really loved his bicycle. He even considered suspension from school a free day to ride his bike. Twenty minutes after he was suspended, he would appear peddling his bicycle back and forth in front of the school. Why did mom reward bratty behavior at school with a privilege that should have been withheld?

Her actions clearly defined the benefits for his behavior: 'If you're a brat, you get to ride your bike longer. If you behave in school, you get to ride your bike less."

Benefits for the wrong actions had been more clearly defined for Tommy than benefits for the right actions. Parents, teachers and administrators couldn't understand why Tommy was such a brat. They created a big problem by rewarding a behavior they didn't want.

We began correcting the mistake by tying the privilege of riding his bike to acceptable behavior at school. First, we clearly defined the benefits for the right actions: Tommy could enjoy the privilege of riding his bike any day he wanted after a day of completed work and satisfactory behavior had been verified by a note from his teacher.

You may think, "Why should he follow the contract?   Won't he just quit?"

No. Children want and love recognition. Consistently reward a behavior and that behavior will occur more frequently.

#3. IGNORE A BEHAVIOR AND THAT BEHAVIOR WILL FADE AWAY

Behavior rewarded will occur more frequently, but you can't merely strengthen new behaviors with a smile and hope the annoying ones go away. It is not that simple.

Two behaviors cannot exist at the same time; they change back and forth until the new behavior dominates. If you want to effectively eliminate kids' unacceptable behavior to make your life easier and your child more responsible, then you must purposefully learn how to ignore the annoying behaviors.

Learning how to ignore annoying behavior isn't as simple as it sounds. Joey's mother wanted to extinguish her son's annoying behavior of teasing and fighting with his sister at mealtime. She decided that Joey's earned reward for acceptable table manners was the privilege of being able to eat with the family. Unacceptable table manners meant that Joey chose to eat alone in the next room. She had to learn to stop nagging him every time she asked him to eat in the next room. Old habits die hard, but the more responsibility she began to take for her own behavior, the less annoying Joey's became. It was working, but Mom wasn't satisfied. Joey still annoyed her with his teasing his sister. Her minister told her not to worry, that Joey was a gift of patience. Mom wanted to scream. I withheld my own sacred comment and suggested I have dinner with them that evening.

Just before dinner was served, while we were sitting at the table and Mom was in the kitchen, Joey cocked his head to one side and glared at his sister. Joey's sister cried out, "Mom, Joey's staring at me again!"

Mom came directly out of the kitchen with a scowl on her face and said, 'Please leave the table and eat in the other room. Your table manners are not acceptable. " She was pointing in the direction of the other room like she was casting him out of the Garden of Eden. The tone of her voice was harsh. As she spoke, she pressed her lips together, wrinkled up her nose, and glared like an insane dog. Now I knew where Joey learned to glare so effectively.

Joey would only display his annoying behavior when he wanted attention. Joey knew all Mom's hot buttons. He'd push and Mom would turn and scowl to such delight that I would have even paid an admission price to see. Mom's scowling behavior gave Joey all the attention he wanted, whenever he demanded it. Mom could scowl to Joey's every delight and not even know it. She had to learn how to become as unemotional as a camera recording events, not reacting to them. When she finally extinguished her own reinforcing behavior, Joey's annoying behavior soon disappeared. Consistently ignore a behavior and that behavior will gradually fade away.

#4. ACTIONS SPEAK LOUDER THAN WORDS

Chris is supposed to go to bed every night at eight o'clock, but usually it's anywhere between eight and nine before he's actually between the sheets with the light turned off. If Mom is in an exceptionally good mood and Chris gives her the appropriate recognition-cuddles up to her and tells her she's the best Mom "I love you Mommy!"-he usually gets to stay up for an additional hour. But if Mom's in a bad mood, then eight o'clock is the law. Chris cuddles but Mom insists. Chris is outraged by this injustice. He begins to scream, yell and cry. If this fails, then Chris creates a tantrum that sets the entire household into emotional turmoil. Sometimes Mom is so tired she gives in to his demands. But sometimes she spanks him. Chris can't understand why he's being picked on. Mom can't understand why she has this hassle every night.

Why such a fuss over a little boy? I asked her if this goes on every night. She said no. Some evenings Chris is a little dear. When Mom works late and comes home after nine o'clock and Chris is still up watching TV, she can yell "Get to bed right now! You know it's past your bedtime!" After a good night kiss, right to bed he goes. No bad feelings for Mom or for Chris. Why? Mom always enforces the bedtime rules when behavior extends beyond the limits. Chris had no ill feelings because when consequences for behavior are consistent, we readily accept the responsibility for our actions. Inconsistency breeds contempt, consistency breeds love.

When she finished telling me about the bedtime drama, she still had bags under her eyes. Remedy? If Chris is conditioned to stay up until nine o'clock, then make nine o'clock bedtime. Not a stir until morning.   Remember, if he can stir a second after nine o'clock, then he can stir an hour. If he fails to follow the bedtime rules, then the next night he goes to bed at eight o'clock. If he fails to follow through at eight o'clock, then the privilege of watching TV is removed the next night. He will test the system to see if you'll do what you say you'll do. His tantrums will escalate. That's OK. His job is to learn The System, yours is to teach him.

On the third night Chris realized he had to be responsible for his behavior if he was to enjoy the privilege of watching television. Mom was consistent with the consequences.

Behavior is affected by action, not words. Regardless of how you feel about it, these laws of behavior exist everyday to determine what you do, how often you do it or can't do it.

My ninety-year-old grandmother always feared she'd be left alone, and because of that fear, she has always felt lonely. Rather than coming out and asking people directly to come over and visit frequently, she feigned illness. She would always tell individual family members, "None of the other family members visit. You're the only one that's good to me. " I believed her. Why should she lie?

I drove 100 miles to see her one evening. When I entered her apartment, six other family members were sitting and visiting. Grandma was sitting in her chair, the center of attention. She was in her glory listening to this, passing that, and laughing at that. The phone rang and she went to the kitchen to answer it and I followed her.

In the living room she was full of life yet when she answered the phone she sounded like a sick, dying woman. When she hung up I said,

"Grandma! I thought you said nobody visits you?"

She looked at me, shrugged her shoulders, rolled her eyes up and raised her hands above her shoulders saying, "When it rains, it pours." It worked while they were young, so why shouldn't it work now? She could have saved herself years of heartache by learning how to communicate her needs like a responsible person rather than like a whining infant, but learning how to get what you want beyond the basics is a learned behavior.

Whenever I meet parents and teachers who report that their child continually whines and pouts I tell them that the child has a winning attitude. That always shocks them. If kids haven't learned how to effectively communicate their needs, whining is a winning attitude. Taking responsible action must be learned because nobody out in the real world is going to just give them what they need and want. Parents may supply their needs while the kids are learning, but the relationship cannot continue. Kids are destined to fend for themselves/ and growing up without having learned how to achieve through responsible action can be a very hopeless and desperate situation-a situation that could even motivate kids to escape.

Children escaping their responsibility have become a national disaster that touches all our lives. They want that quick fix to wash all those blues away. From rural farm towns to major cities, kids are turning to drugs and alcohol, running away from home, and committing suicide at an alarming rate. The story of a troubled child doesn't merit the evening news anymore; it's the neighborhood gossip.

Learning how the game operates isn't easy but it is an easier alternative to some of the escape routes our children are choosing today. It is a learned behavior, not an inborn privilege. Raising children for success is teaching children how to become responsible for their actions. It's not an option; it's mandatory.

A mother came to me concerned about her daughter Jennifer, who was about eleven months old at the time.

"Every time I take something away from her that she shouldn't be playing with, Jennifer immediately falls on the floor face down and begins to cry like she's in pain," she said. It's rather like a tantrum. I don't know where she learned that behavior. She's not around other children, and she's doing it more and more. "

I told the mother that her child falling down on the ground to get what she wants isn't a new behavior. Mom had been servicing this same behavior since Jennifer first stood up in the crib, fell down, and she rushed over to hug the pain away saying, "There, there. Would you like a bottle?" The attention and the bottle were the child's reward for falling down. Later in life, when kids are two, three, four, or even six years old, they are still throwing themselves down on the floor in the market or in the kitchen because they couldn't have the ice cream. They are merely practicing behaviors that were winning at one time, and well approved.

"The behavior is acceptable," I said. "The behavior is a winning attitude because she learned that when she falls on the floor she gets what she wants. That's all right. Jennifer is practicing a winning action and a winning attitude. When she was an infant, it was important for her, but now it's time to move on and grow out of it. There is nothing wrong with it. Allow her to do it, but don't reward her for it. If she doesn't receive anything for the action, the behavior will fade away. It has to. How long would you continue working and performing certain behaviors if you ceased getting paid for them at your job? Not too long. A child's job isn't any different. After all, learning how to grow up is their job. If someone is not reinforced for a specific behavior, that behavior will not continue because it's not getting them what they want."

"But sometimes Jennifer has tantrums while other people are visiting and it's difficult to ignore."

"What do you do when she does that?" I asked.

"I either give Jennifer what she wants or spank her."

Either way, Mom was supplying Jennifer with her desires-attention-just like she used to get when she fell down in the crib. I suggested that if the behavior becomes so noisy and obnoxious that it can't be ignored, just pick her up and put her in her room. Remove her from the room, and let her perform elsewhere. Admonishing and attention are the same thing to a child. Jennifer was able to draw her mother's attention away from everything and everyone to concentrate solely on her. She got just what she wanted-her mother's attention-just like she always had.

Children do not learn new behaviors by magic. Each behavior must be learned. Teach kids directly what they need to know. First, evaluate the behavior for current appropriateness. At one time the child's behavior served a purpose, now it's time to move on. Cease recognizing that behavior because it is no longer needed. Next, teach your children new behaviors that will get them what they want. What they want is what we all want: WHAT EVERYBODY WANTS IS TO HAVE WHAT THEY WANT. Teach your kids to get what they want through purposeful, responsible action.

Children can't learn something new unless somebody shows them how to do it. Oh, they could learn by trial and error, but why leave success to chance? Why waste your precious time and their youth when you could be enjoying the time together? Children need good models for success. Don't waste your time enduring childish behaviors and their time trying to figure out how to get what they want when you could both get what you want.

•Teach them directly what they need to know so they can take personal responsibility for their actions.

•Teach your children directly by modeling, show and tell.

•Teach care for toys.

•Teach them how to talk by using correct

sentence structure. Don't babble back to them like a child. They already know how to do that. They need to learn how to talk like adults.

*When they are learning how to stand up,

teach them how to put one leg under the other. Teach them how to reach up and grab the edge of the chair or crib to steady themselves.

•Show them how to sit quietly.

•Expect nothing unless it has been taught. Train them for success. Give kids the same training you'd expect to get at a new job.

•Teach them directly.

When Jennifer tired of the tantrums because they weren't rewarded, her mom picked her up and asked her what she wanted. Then she told her how to act and showed her how.

"Next time that happens all you have to do is come over to me, touch my finger to get my attention and tell me what you need and you will have it. "

Then she physically walked Jennifer through the steps, moving her hands and legs through the motions with the reward. She taught her how to ask for her needs.

Learning how to ask, to seek out even at such a basic level of need, automatically begins to put a child in the top five percent of successful people. It is the beginning of being personally responsible for their actions and wants.

Later Mom reported the tantrums quickly faded away and the new behavior took it's place. At fourteen months Jennifer now walks into the room and touches Mom's finger and then asks for something.   Some adults should be so advanced.

Teach your kids behaviors they will need in order to get the things they want. If you do not like a particular behavior, then use the laws of behavior to change what you're doing to get what you want. Teach personal responsibility and reap big rewards.

3

The Laws of Success

We raise kids for success by understanding and teaching them the laws of success.

The number one law of success is the law of cause and effect. It is predictable and irreversible. Knowing how to use the law, kids can attract success and happiness. Ignorance of the law can result in boredom, frustration, and failure, which can lead to fear, drugs, and suicide.

#1. WHATEVER YOU HAVE, THAT'S WHAT YOU WANT

Not knowing how to play the game of life does not exclude anyone. You've heard kids say to each other or even to their parents, "I didn't know!" as an excuse for not taking personal responsibility for some action. That's an artificial system.   Life doesn't operate that way. In the real game of life there are no second chances. Ignorance of the law is no excuse.

You can't be excluded from the game. You're not observers. You are the major players. There's only one way to be excused from life on this earth and that's to stop breathing (an alternative too many kids are choosing today). This may sound depressing, but the good news is that the game has no losers. WHATEVER YOU PLAY FOR, THAT'S WHAT YOU GET. The answer is always, "Yes!" You're a winner every time because you always get exactly what you create for yourself. What you decide to play for is up to you.

Many people think that life is like a slot machine: they merely pull the handle and hope they win. Life is a-do-it-to-yourself proposition, not a hopeless out of control gamble. The slot machine has no glass covering the spinning fruit. You can reach in, stop the fruit, and arrange them any way you want.

Wherever you are right now, look around you. You are sitting amongst the spoils of your efforts. See your kids in all their glory, because you can thank nobody for them but yourself. If you like where you are, then don't change a thing, just keep doing what you're doing. But if you would like to change a few things, then take a closer look at how the game is played.

Regardless of your personal feelings, kids need and desire a concrete world. There is no such thing as a bad child. They want to know that their persistence will help them achieve in the directions they desire to go. They want to be like adults. That's the whole reason behind their daily activities. Watch them. They play games: foursquare, Monopoly, kickball. Every thinkable game has structured, well balanced rules that, if followed, will allow them to win. If the game does not have structure and rules that allow them to win, they lose interest very quickly. All of it is built around order. Kids all want to know exactly what the rules are, and if players are cheating, the other players call them on it. Sometimes kids cheat on purpose just to see if the game will be honest, and if they're called on their cheating, they smile. They know what they've done, and they're delighted they've been held responsible. They want order; they want structure.

Kids need to know that their behavior is going to have an effect. They must experience how the game of life operates and come to know accountability. If you deny kids this freedom, then you're not allowing them to truly enjoy the gift; instead, you'll force them to live life like so many adults, spending their precious time trying to figure out how to play the game rather than enjoying it.

A structured, disciplined environment is a child's security. As they get older, they'll see that the world is structured and disciplined just like the laws of nature. If they grow up without the discipline and structure, they'll have no direction because their actions will only have a random effect. It will be like playing a monopoly game with no rules. Games without structure create great anxiety, and anxiety makes an unhappy child.

#2. KIDS MUST LEARN TO EARN

When kids learn the laws of success they will become masters of achievement: they will be in control and know how to get what they want. In order to get what they want beyond the basic necessities they had as children, you must literally teach them that everything they get beyond the basics they must earn. Kids must learn to earn. As adults, they will have to earn everything, basic necessities and luxuries.

Children find this difficult to learn because as toddlers everything was given to them. Now as they get older, the game appears to be changing for them. It demands they move beyond the basics and learn new behaviors to get what they want. Their needs become more complex as they get older, and in fact the older they get, the more it seems everything must be earned.

This is the cruelest reality for adolescence. They just can't sit parked in front of the television and expect their grade-point average to rise or a new car in the driveway. The old behaviors that used to get them what they wanted - whining or crying for parents to fill their needs just don't work anymore. For teenagers / anything beyond basic food on the table and roof over their heads must be earned.

Learning to earn actually begins at the toddling age when children begin to take their first steps and begin acquiring that long sought after independence: being able to fetch for themselves, to dress themselves, to feed themselves. They strive for it; they are even willing to risk bruised knees and frustration for it. With this independence, however, also comes a new responsibility that they must earn what they get. As children grow, they must learn new communication skills of knowing how to ask and accepting delayed gratification, rather than whining and pouting and expecting the world to stop so their wishes can be granted immediately. They must learn how to play the game according to the grown-up world where everything must be earned unless, of course, they want to remain dependent on someone else all their lives. If they remain dependent, social invalids, they'll never know how to take control of their lives and will live in bitterness, gloom and frustration because they will never learn how to get what they want. If they are to learn, you must teach them.   It won't just happen by itself.

Nothing works by itself. So often parents and teachers come back to me after trying a specific program saying, "I don't think this is going to work!" My standard response is, "Of course it doesn't work. "

Or a parent or teacher reports that the children aren't doing specific tasks or not acting responsibly.

"They're not supposed to, " I say. "They don't know how. "

Children are born into this world with all the capabilities for success. Their minds are the finest computers ever produced; yet the mind does absolutely nothing unless they know how to make it work. An untrained animal, man or beast, is of no use to itself or anybody else. If they sit and vegetate then the computer vegetates. If they input information by teaching it how to work- mathematics, languages, good table manners, how to communicate, how to act to get the things they want then their computer can begin to work for them. But until then, nothing will work.

Kids weren't born into this world to have things work for them; they were born into this world to make things work. By making things work, they become the person they need to be. If they want to learn how to play a particular sport, trade, skill, or whatever, they learn by finding out the rules of how to make it work, hi the game of tennis, they have to begin by learning the rules of the game and then practice, practice, practice. As they begin to make it work, to be able to exercise intelligent control, they become a better tennis player. They become the person they want to become by learning to make things work.

Once you realize that kids must learn to earn and life isn't a game of chance, you realize that to get the results you have to pay the price. Everybody must work; everybody must pay. The sooner children learn that they need to take the responsibility to do the work, then the sooner the game of life is going to reward them for their efforts.

Getting results by taking responsible action can be compared to a farmer and his crop. A farmer can go to an open field and say, "I want this field to yield a crop of corn. " But the wishing alone does not create the corn. You have to go in and plow the field and plant the corn in the spring, properly. If you want the yield, you have to pay the price.

For the modern television generation, this seems like a nightmare. The idea that life isn't turning out like a television miniseries is difficult enough to accept without adding the idea that they have to work for everything they want. Why a mere whine or a pout used to get immediate results.

The act of planting isn't all there is to it. They must also be persistent and patient. During the summer months they have to care for the field. Water and weed; water and weed. They have to nurture it through the fall harvest in order to get the rewards from their work. They have to pay the price.

The two behaviors that kill success quicker than anything are impatience and greed - wanting results from your labor too quickly without waiting for them to mature. Little children do not understand delayed gratification. Why should they? As small children they always received their wants immediately. At the mere squeak of their voice Mom and Dad came running. Now they have to WAIT! If they want to have what they want, they'll have to learn patience and persistence. They have to be able to stick around long enough to get the results. They can't dig up the seed everyday to see if it's bearing fruit. They can't expect to learn how to ride a bike the first day. To learn how to walk they have to crawl. If they want a lot then they'll have to learn how to save a little at a time.

"Patience my child. Patience, and it will come. You can't expect too much too soon. You have to watch it grow day by day," my father would say after we planted the melons. My broker used the same words when I continually checked my mutual fund (Oh Lord give me patience, and give it to me now!)

Imagine kids learning at an early age that in order to get what they want they'll have to learn how to work and save to achieve. How fantastic! The joy of work is taking responsible action, planting the field to get the yield. The joy of responsibility is to be there in the spring, to care for it in the summer, to harvest it in the fall. The joy of sticking it out is getting results.

If kids are not responsible then they will not get the rewards. And who do they blame? It doesn't matter because they themselves are left without the reward. They can blame their parents, the schools, the government, the weather, they can stand naked in the field and whine at the wind, but that kind of labor does nothing for the results, because whether they like it or whether they don't, the law of cause and effect still applies. If they don't have the down payment because they weren't responsible enough to work and save, then they won't get the house. There just ain't no free lunch. Kids must learn to earn.

What happens if you stop working? Whatever you were working on gradually begins to deteriorate. But that's how the game is played: nothing works by itself until you decide to make it work, and then you must continue to make it work. Only through work can you achieve and only if you're achieving can you be happy. If you want kids to be happy and have the self-respect of knowing how to get what they want, then teach them also how to deserve.

#3. HAPPY KIDS ARE DESERVING KIDS

Do kids always have to be working? They can rest, but the rest must be deserved. Only through work can they rest. Rest is a reward.   In order to enjoy it, kids must earn it Rewards without work have no satisfaction. It has no purpose and therefore cannot be deserved. The surest way to create discontent is to reward without labor.

I see this happen all the time when teachers and parents reward kids before they have completed their work. You can't reward kids who don't deserve it and expect them to be happy. The end result is discontent and anxiety. Existence in that state of mind too long will trigger revolt. Revolt against a nation is called revolution. Revolt within yourself is called suicide. If you don't operate the way life is supposed to operate you will cease to play the game. It's incredible to believe that if kids are receiving their wants without work, they'll be unhappy. "I give them everything they want and they're still unhappy. I give up," are the words of a frustrated parent.

Imagine the game of life as a card game or a home entertainment game. You sit down to play and your opponents say, "You win" before the game even begins. What satisfaction is there? None. How often will you play that game? Never. It has no purpose. So why would the game of life be any different? If the game ceases to have purpose then why shouldn't we quit that game too? The problem is that kids do quit.   Our kids are quitting all the time.

Life responds to those who deserve, not need. Any other system is artificial and is doomed to fail. If children who aren't deserving are rewarded, then you are teaching them that they cannot achieve through responsible action. If children's actions cannot determine their direction and destination, then you are not raising them for success, but rather how to be neurotic. Sometimes they get their rewards and sometimes they don't. If you can't have good dreams, then you'll have nightmares. Whimsy and moods, regardless of their intentions, don't raise happy responsible kids, but rather depressed and irresponsible ones. It's the law of cause and effect. When kids haven't earned their rewards but you reward them anyway, you are killing them with kindness. You teach them that they have little control over their lives. They are like slaves who can only whimper, whine, and hope. These kids live day-today with very little happiness, only a moody bitterness waiting to explode. Moody kids are like tantruming babies. Neither knows how to win through responsible action, but they can learn. Rewards must be deserved.

Farmers are among the few people who truly understand that there is an unwritten contract of responsibility: if you plant, you will reap; if you don't plant, you won't reap. Only those who plant shall reap, not those who need. If a farmer doesn't take the necessary steps of planting in the spring, all the tears in the fall won't turn that field into a deserving crop. City dwellers may look at the situation with skepticism and say, "What if someone really needs? Doesn't that count?"

Not in the game of life. That is an artificial system that teaches failure and regret. The game of life says that if people are in need, then they must learn how to deserve. If they don't like the arrangements of learning how to deserve before they can receive, then they're just going to have to live in misery.

The game of life applies to everybody, not just the farmer. Regardless of where they live, everybody must work and everybody must pay in order to reap rewards. If children don't learn the necessary steps of taking responsibility for their own actions early in life, all the years of government assistance won't change them into deserving adults. Needs have nothing to do with it. Life responds only to those who deserve, not to those who need.

I knew a farmer who lived on a small farm with his five sons. He worked his boys strenuously. A local who knew the farmer and the particulars concerning his farm said, "You don't have to work the boys as hard as you do to raise a crop."

The farmer paused for a moment He looked down at the ground and stirred the dirt with the tip of his shoe, then looked up, met the other man's eyes with a grin and said, "I'm not raising a crop. I'm raising five boys." That man was my father.

Maybe we weren't meant to dwell in cities. Maybe it was easier in the past when over ninety percent of the population had to learn how to be responsible for their actions or starve to death! If you plant, you will reap; if you don't plant, you won't reap. Being away from the land requires a more purposeful earning.

#4. KIDS OBEY THE RULES FOR THE SAME REASONS THEY BREAK THEM

Systems that are unnatural will ultimately fail. If you don't get the pay you won't do the work. That's the major cause of revolutions, whether the revolution is in a household, in a school or in a nation. Artificial systems do not last.

In a place of business an employee who does the work and does not get the pay does not continue working. Kids who do the work and do not get the pay do not continue working. A business prospers when those who receive its merchandise or service benefit. It is inherently satisfying. It's natural. A household will prosper the same way. If a system fails to reward action, love is not the end result, but defiance. Children obey the rules for the same reason they break them. When benefits for the right actions are clearly given, you get conformity, not defiance.

A few years ago I was working with a single parent of four boys. She was a legal secretary and her job demanded that she jet out of town at a moment's notice. This wonderful mama's lifestyle should have been a parenting magazine's classic example of the causes of home problems. Not so. I asked her about this and she said they learned responsibility at a very young age.

She never nagged them; she simply didn't have the time. If she was called out of town, she gave the kids ten minutes to be in the car and ready for the baby sitter. If they dawdled, then half naked and toy less into the car they went. They learned quickly. If they did the work they got the pay. It was the same system their mother had to live with. Her attitude was encouraging because the consequences were determined by the child's own actions. Nothing artificial.

If her children didn't get their act together in time then they didn't enjoy the stay at the baby sitter's as much. When children know they are in complete control of their environment they learn quickly. Negative results aren't undeserved punishment, but a natural consequence of personal selection like turning on the cold water accidentally in the shower. Who do you blame? It doesn't matter. What matters is who gets the cold shower. They learn quickly when they're in complete control.

Allow kids to be accountable. Don't hide success from them. Why make the game of life frustrating when it can be fun? Don't protect them from accountability; create an opportunity for it.

The legal secretary created the system that governed her household. I praised her on a wonderful family. She thanked me and said, "We work at it daily.   But what's the alternative?"

Parents can be too quick to protect their children from the natural consequences of their own actions. I think parents tend to see natural consequences more as punishment than as a natural effect which the child chose to cause. Whenever I work with kids in the home or in the school, I always make sure that their chores and obligations are defined for them and their privileges are conditional payment for work completed, whenever that task is completed. The privilege is a natural consequence. In my classroom, children need to complete a specified amount of work. If they choose not to be productive and complete it within the given amount of time, they have the option of taking it home to complete. If they arrive the next day with the work incomplete, then they have chosen to remain after hours to complete the necessary work. It's no different than the real concrete world of accountability they'll be asked to participate in as adults.

You live with the consequences for your actions and reactions. That's accountability. It goes on working whether you like it or accept it. It's like the law of gravity. Whether you accept it or not, the law doesn't change. Gravity goes on working. You can use its force to reach out to the universe and build a better life or you can choose to be ignorant and live like ants crawling under its pressure. The better you understand accountability, the easier it is to be effective and productive. You can complain and blame whoever you desire, but ultimately you are responsible because you must live with the consequences. Those who do the work get the pay, those who get the pay do the work. That's the law.

#5. KIDS CAN ACT ANY WAY YOU WANT THEM TO ACT

If kids are going to learn how to play the game then they'll need good models.

Children conform to the values to which they are exposed. If they're exposed to good values, they'll have good values. If they're exposed to bad values, they'll be bad. It all depends on the parent. Kids can act any way you want them to act. They look up to their parents as mirrors to their little world.

Are you being good models? Are you taking personal responsibility for your actions by working a regular job and making responsible payments for your home, car and daily necessities, but raising your kids in a completely different direction by giving them things rather than having them earn them? What are you teaching them? WHATEVER YOU PLANT, THAT'S WHAT YOU GET.

If parents plant the seeds of bad habits they won't get good habits. If you plant peas, you'll get peas. If you plant carrots, you'll get carrots. If you plant corn, you won't get watermelons! This may sound very naive and quite basic, but I think some parents are ignorant of what they plant and expect to get a luscious crop of good habits. I call these seeds of defeat and what they harvest is frustration. Some parents are so perplexed that they just sit around murmuring, "No, no, no, no," while their children peddle circles around them in their noise-laden car at full bore. Solution? They're the ones that bought the car; they can remove the car. Whatever you plant, that's what you get.

When benefits for the wrong actions are clearly given, you are planting bad seeds.

I remember watching a movie years ago called *The Bad Seed*. The movie was about a little girl who would perform malicious acts to eliminate people to get what she wanted (Hollywood gives birth to yet another myth). In one particular scene, the little girl would spend hours mesmerized by a music box.

The elderly lady noticed how much the little girl loved the music box and said, "When I die you can have the box."

You guessed it. Soon after the elderly lady was lying at the bottom of the stairs, in grotesque detail. The little girl was standing at the top of the stairs stroking the music box with a grin on her face that would make your skin crawl. Is there such a thing as a bad seed? At times it seems that way.   But no child is born a bad seed.

All children are born to win. Unfortunately, they are often ignored until they do something annoying. If children are playing quietly, when are they usually recognized? When they begin to whine. If kids are drawing at the kitchen table, when do you attend to them? When they begin drawing on the table. When do parents usually attend to their children's school work? When they're not doing it. Parents forget their kids are even around until they disturb the status quo.

If you don't like the effect you're getting, then you need to change the cause. In other words, if you don't like the harvest, then you have to change what you're planting. If children are whining, moody, or displaying unacceptable behaviors every time they want something and you determine that's not the kind of relationship you want, then you need to change the cause to get the desired effect. If you don't change the cause then you'll just keep getting more of what you already have.

I was counseling a young family that lived in Hawaii. They had a three-year-old boy and a five-year-old girl. Mom was concerned about her five-year-old daughter Tina. She called me on the phone and said she had taken Tina to the supermarket as usual. They were in the fruit and vegetable department when Mom went over to the grape bin and she tasted a grape to determine whether she wanted to purchase them. She also gave one to Tina, who automatically tasted it, just like Mom.

"Do you think Mommy should buy these?"

Tina smacked her kips and said, "Fucking good," in a loud, clear voice.

Mom was shocked as other shoppers turned to stare. She didn't know what to do, so she picked Tina up and rushed out of the store. Mom didn't allow Tina to watch television or play with her friends that day.

When she called me, Mom was a little frustrated. She felt guilty about punishing the child. "What do you think was the cause of this behavior?" I asked.

"I have no idea," said Mom.

"Where would Tina hear that kind of language?"

"Well, my husband sometimes uses that expression, but only in humor."

I told her that whether in humor or not, that's probably the cause. "Do you like the effect you are getting?"

"No!" she exclaimed.

"Great. Wasn't that simple. Just change the cause and you'll change the effect. The next time you taste your food, especially grapes, choose a positive phrase to describe the flavor. Use a phrase like "this tastes perfect." Or "these are remarkable."

Stop using the language you don't want the kids to use and begin choosing the language you want them to use. To become successful, children must become the type of people that attract the cooperation of other people. They can't attract more than what they are. Their thoughts and actions will determine their direction. The way they walk, the way they talk, and even the quality and integrity of the people they associate with will determine their success. Children can't be more than what they choose to associate with. What kind of life do you want your kids to attract? Who your kids are with today will determine what they will be tomorrow. My aunt always said, "Show me a person's friends and I'll show you the person."

I told Tina's Mom not to worry about the behavior. There is no such thing as bad behavior. All behavior is good; it just may not be appropriate for a particular time and place. There is a time and place for everything. Even violence and violent language had its place in time of war. But I don't think grape tasting is an act of war. Using the language "fucking good" isn't bad behavior, but it may not be appropriate in the supermarket.

How successful will Tina be later in life using that kind of descriptive language? What kind of impression will that leave upon her teachers and her playmate's parents? Peer group will determine her direction very early in life. What kind of peer group do you think that behavior will attract? Kids will attract those kinds of people that are most like themselves. As a parent would you want your child spending time with children who use that kind of language? The point is, don't consider her behavior as bad, but rather ask yourself is that the success oriented direction you want her to go?

Later Tina's Mom called and said the solution was so simple. "Just change the cause to get the effect we want. Now we're moving in the right direction. I can take her to the store! When we know what to do, we can laugh at the situation."

Just before she hung up she said, "Jeff, the more I know about what I need to do, the easier it is on a day-to-day basis. It's such a pleasure to be able to enjoy the relationship of watching them grow and explore. I used to be so afraid wondering if I was doing the right things. I was always so afraid of making them unhappy, like I was hurting their development. But now we know what to do and why we're doing it. Even more than that, we found out that as we learn how to raise them, we're changing too. We do have to change some of our habits, and as we change we're finding we're becoming more successful in other areas. It just seems to be snowballing. Everything used to be so hard and now it's so simple.   I feel a little stupid." I laughed and said, "It's hard to play any game when you don't know what's expected."

She didn't like what she was planting so she simply uprooted the weed and started with fresh seed. A simple solution. No mysteries. Whatever you plant, that's what you get.

#6. KIDS DO THINGS FOR THEIR OWN REASONS

All behavior is voluntary. People do things for their own reasons.

One particular day a parent came to the classroom concerned about why her child was being kept after school, "Forced to miss the early bus."

I told the mother that the question she should be asking is not why we are doing this to the child, but rather why the child is keeping the teacher after school on a beautiful afternoon to discuss who is responsible for his actions? All behavior is voluntary. Kids are in more control than we like to admit.

She looked at me.   "What do you mean?"

"Well, you know that your son has the opportunity of completing his work within a certain amount of time here at school and even at home. What was your boy doing last night?"

"After dinner he watched television until it was time to go to bed."

I laughed. "In other words, your son chose to watch television rather than completing his work. Not bad. I guess I probably would have chosen to get the privilege rather than do the work too. That's really OK. But now he has created the situation that forced you to drive all the way over here to take responsibility for his actions while he enjoyed watching television. 'What are his responsibilities' is the question we should be asking ourselves."

She stopped me and said, "Well, when he gets home, he's really going to get it!"

"No," I said. "Being here completing his work isn't punishment. It's merely the option he chose. Normally he would be home enjoying the privilege of playing with his friends, but instead he chose to be here completing his daily responsibilities. It's really no different from your obligations of daily work. If you choose to spend more time at work because you haven't been as productive as you should, that's OK. It's being accountable. The natural consequence is that you enjoy less time at home, not punishment. The system for kids should be the same. Now if you would like to help your boy become more responsible, then I'd suggest making the privilege of watching television each night conditional. Make a written contract that's agreeable to both of you. Make the home privilege conditional upon completing his assigned work within a specified amount of time. You can either teach him directly now or he can learn it later by accident. But he will learn it, so why not now?"

She understood. Her frown changed to a smile. Her son came out into the corridor. He thought he was going to get to go home. He even had his jacket on and his books in hand.

Mom looked at him and smiled. "We'll see you at home later on," she said, then turned and walked out.

The boy looked at me, bewildered. He was shocked that his mom didn't take him home. He had counted on her taking the responsibility.

The situation happened less frequently. His work was always completed on time and he always had a good attitude. Later on I learned that he and Mom agreed that if he didn't make the early bus home, then he chose not to watch television that night. The action wasn't a punishment; it was merely a natural consequence that he controlled. If you don't do the work, you don't get the pay. As time went on, his success became more frequent.   He was taking control, and when he enters the job market, that same success will carry over because he learned how to be accountable for his behavior at an early age.

Being successful means taking the responsibility to do the work.

It is a learned behavior. Kids can't be expected to do what they haven't learned. Are you giving things to them rather than having them earn them? Are you allowing accountability to affect their lives now as it is going to affect them as adults? They have to be able to operate the way life operates. You can't protect kids from life and then expect them to be able to handle it. That's an artificial system destined for misery for both parent and child. Those who do the work will get the pay and those who get the pay will do the work.

The law creates a concrete world. Order is security. Discipline is freedom. Don't be afraid to create an environment that allows kids to operate the way life is supposed to operate. Kids not only can handle it, they desire it. They want to be in control. Your job is to teach them how.

So when you look at cause and effect, consider that kids do want to know that their behavior does have an effect, that it does have a direction, and it is putting them where they need to be. If it is not, then something needs to change. They will change it or you will change it. Either way, a change will take place.

4

Kids Can Change

#1. CHILDREN ARE CREATURES OF HABIT

How do you change all the uninspired, unhappy kids into inspired and happy ones? If you want your kids to live successfully, not merely a basic hand to mouth existence, they have to be willing to form habit patterns that are successful.

Habit patterns are necessary for success. Could you imagine that if every time you had to tie your shoes you had to think about the process, relearning each time as you did when you were a child? The first time you sat behind the wheel of a clutch driven car, it probably felt like an impossible skill to learn when you looked down and saw the three pedals and only two feet. Through practice, habit patterns allow you to learn skills and not have to relearn them

Now you can tie your shoes and drive an automobile without the activities consuming all your time and attention, allowing you to move on with your life in other directions.   We are creatures of habit.

Children need to acquire successful habit patterns. Kids need to learn the skills and behaviors that will enable them to get what they want through responsible action. They don't need skills and behaviors to become adults, that change is inevitable.

#2. CHOOSING SUCCESSFUL HABIT PATTERNS

How do you know which habit patterns are successful? People fall into different habit patterns. Successful people do certain things. Unsuccessful people do certain things. Find out what unsuccessful people do and don't do it! Find out what successful people do and do it!

When looking at children's habit patterns, I tell parents to ask themselves two questions: #1. Is this a habit pattern that will help children to get what they want through responsible action? #2. If all the kid's were to act like this, as children or adults, would it be OK?

If you cannot answer, "yes" to both questions, then it's not a successful habit pattern. If you can answer "Yes", then it is a good habit pattern. Successful people do certain things.   Become a student of human habit patterns, and then pick and choose the ones you need and let the others go.

Ryan's mom called me, concerned about her son's behavior at home and at school.

"He's not progressing in school, "she said. "I can't get him to do anything at home anymore. I used to be able to give him special desserts and treats if he'd work, but even that's not working any more."

When I visited her, I observed that although Ryan was a normal, handsome twelve-year-old boy, he was still using the behaviors of an infant to get attention and approval from Mom and probably the teacher. When he wanted something or he desired to play, he would run through the house dancing, skipping, hiding things, and sneaking up behind adults yelling, "Hey sucker!"

These behaviors worked at five years old, but because of his maturity, which requires him to communicate his needs more directly, the behaviors were now causing stress. Mom was still reinforcing the behaviors by responding to them. As a remedy, I gave Mom a quick rule of thumb.

"Your child's behavior should be no different than any responsible adults," I said. "If you wonder how to determine responsible behaviors, just ask yourself, 'Is this behavior acceptable in the working world? Will it get him where he needs to go?' If the answer is no, stop the behavior right when he does it, then tell him how to act. Say 'whenever you don't know something or want something/this is how you ask' - Then tell him. Exactly. Word for word. Have him repeat what you say.

When Ryan's Mom was in the room, I asked Ryan if he was going outside.

He didn't answer.

I asked again.

"What? What'd yah say? You talkin' to me?" He pointed with his finger toward his chest, real cutesy.

"Ryan," I said, "Put your hands down. If I ask you a question just answer me. You'll always have my attention."

"You talkin' to me?" he smirked.

"Stop," I said. I repeated my instruction again, in a calm voice as if I was talking to a friend. Then I said, "Repeat what I said. "

He did.

"Thank you," I said. "Are you going outside?"

"Yes. Why?"

"Will you please stop at the store?"

He smiled and said, "Yes", just like an adult.

The next day I asked Ryan another question concerning his activities and he started to react cutesy again. Immediately he stopped himself, like he was catching himself from falling, and answered me properly. I responded with a smile, my attention and my approval.

Ryan does have acceptable behaviors and I told Mom to respond to them.   In doing so she was automatically picking the ones she wanted and letting the others go. Whatever you recognize, expect to get more of it.

#3. TEACHING KIDS TO GET WHAT THEY WANT

To form successful habit patterns means kids must be willing to change what's not working to what does work. If they want to become successful, they must be willing to change. To change what they're doing, however, means to change habit patterns, and creatures of habit don't like to change. Change takes effort and effort is work. Once they find something that works, it's easier to keep on doing what they're doing than to learn something new. After all, why should they learn something new if their present behaviors get them what they want? If your present behaviors get you what you want, I doubt very much you'd want to change. Change is only necessary when what you're doing doesn't get you what you want.

If tantruming gets children what they want then there is no reason to change. From children to adults, they say, "Why I've been doing it this way all my life and I'm not about to change!" And why should they? As young children their wants and needs have always been the responsibility of others. The basic behaviors they had at birth had always proved successful. One good cry would usually do the trick. But crying for their needs won't always get them what they want.   WE MUST TEACH THEM THAT ONLY THROUGH CHANGE CAN THEY GET WHAT THEY WANT.

Adults and children usually aren't willing to change what they're doing unless what they're doing no longer gets them what they want. When that happens you usually say, "I have a problem". But that's only when the major problem occurs. All major problems have minor beginnings. The real problem started when they decided not to operate the way life is supposed to operate. You can't merely choose to stop changing and expect things to remain the same. Life doesn't work that way. Change is inevitable. Change will happen whether you like it or not.

Change will occur when the difference between what you have and what you want becomes great enough then it will erupt like a volcano. Ryan's mom was still concerned about his reading problem and his constant misbehaving in school.

I told her not to be overly concerned about the reading. "Reading may not be his strength, but finding the proper instructor can correct the problem. It's a skill that can be learned. It needs practice and work. That's something kids don't like to do. If he didn't learn discipline early in reading, then he'll need to learn it now, but it will be more difficult for him now because he has gradually acquired misbehavior to compensate for his poor reading skills. "

When Ryan was younger, if he couldn't read he could act coy, shy and cutesy and still acquire the attention and approval he wanted. Now, however, those social behaviors aren't getting him the attention and approval like they used to. Since he can't get attention and approval by displaying his ability to read like the other students can, he misbehaves to cover up his inabilities by using the same behaviors he is accustomed to using to attract attention. Now it's not considered coy, cutesy and shy-now it's a Behavior Problem.

Ryan's behavior problems are an outgrowth of his using old behaviors to acquire attention and approval for himself. The situation has always existed, but now it has evolved into a major problem because his needs-attention and approval-are the same as when he was younger, but acceptable methods for acquiring his needs have changed while his behavior has not.

As a young child Ryan's behaviors and needs were equal. There was no reason for change. But now the distance between his behavior and his needs has become great enough to create a problem and a need for change.

As the distance between Ryan's behavior and what he wants and needs becomes greater, the greater the stress, the bigger the problem. When this happens, Mom has a crisis.

Ryan has been allowed not to acquire his academic skills by compensating his shortcomings with cutesy behaviors that were reinforced. But it's NO BIG DEAL. All kids go through it. It's called growing up and it's usually harder on the parents than on the kids. Mom merely needs to make the behavior and the needs equal by teaching Ryan directly what he needs to do.

Change will only occur when the difference between what you have and what you want becomes great enough.

All major problems have minor beginnings. It's like never doing any minor repairs on your home. The minor problems can be overlooked until your house begins to fall down-major problem. Not fixing a leaky pipe until it rots the wall-major problem. Listening to your kids whine just a little each day about something, or watching them not always doing their best job, or some days not getting their work done at all, until one day all these minor behaviors explode into outright refusal to cooperate - major problem. The difference between their behaviors and what they need or want begin to grow apart.

How do kids become uninspired and unhappy? Most people wait for major problems to happen before they're willing to change.

People with problems never have the time to get what they want because they always have problems. After a while they quit trying. They just shrink their wants to match what they're getting. They gradually become unhappy and uninspired. KIDS BECOME UNINSPIRED AND UNHAPPY NOT BECAUSE THEY DONT HAVE WHAT THEY WANT, BUT BECAUSE THEY DON'T KNOW HOW TO GET FROM WHERE THEY ARE TO WHAT THEY WANT.

Life is merely a game. It's not a question of whether you want to play; it's a question of what you want to win. The problem is that most people know what they want to win but they don't know how to play the game. Their ignorance forces them to live in daily discouragement. Once they're discouraged, bingo, the Pike Syndrome catches another fish before they even start the game.

What's the Pike Syndrome? Scientists did an experiment where they took a pike and put him into a large fish tank with an ample supply of minnows. Whenever the pike became hungry, he merely had to open his mouth and snap up a minnow. Then the scientists put a glass jar over the pike. They wanted to determine how long the pike would continue to hit the glass jar striking out after minnows before he became discouraged. For quite a while the pike would strike out after the minnows and crash into the jar. This behavior continued for quite some time until the pike gradually did it less and less. When the pike finally stopped, the scientists removed the jar. The pike sank to the bottom of the tank and just lay there.   Once again, with the jar removed, the minnows started swimming freely around the pike, even brushing up against his mouth. Not once did the pike strike out. The scientists' intention was to teach the pike the rules of their game - when the jar is down, relax; when the jar is removed, feast. But the pike just lay on the bottom of the tank and literally starved to death. Minnows were everywhere for the taking, and the pike just starved to death.

So many kids give up before they really even get started just because they don't know how to play the game. They become a pike starving to death with minnows everywhere.

You were born for success and happiness, not discouragement. If you want to win, child or adult, you have to know how to play the game. Keep it simple and operate the way life is supposed to operate.

Telltale signs of uninspired kids: tired, moody, critical, whining, unhappy, poor grades, can't find anything to do, dabbling with drugs, misbehaving at school, being rude, cussing, talking back, destructive, no respect for the personal belongings of others. Yet these uninspired kids were born to win. How do you make all uninspired, unhappy kids inspired and happy ones? You teach them that through change they can get what they want.

#4. LEARNING BY ACCIDENT AND LEARNING ON PURPOSE

How children learn will determine their success. There are two ways to learn: learning by accident and learning on purpose. Learning on purpose is more effective, but more people tend to choose to learn by accident. They hope they win the game before their time runs out.

Learning by accident is a kind of groping through the dark hoping for a move in the right direction. Learning by accident gets the job done, but it takes too long. How much of your precious time do you want to spend groping in the dark learning by accident?

There is another way of learning. It's called learning on purpose. It also gets the job done, gets it done faster, gets you moving in the right direction, gets you to your destination.

There's no wrong way to do something. Everyone will eventually arrive at a destination, the question is: "Where?" There isn't a right way and a wrong way, there is a right way and a long way. Which way do you choose? It's merely a choice. If you don't like what you're doing or where you are then change it. The problem with most people is they spend their entire lives learning how not to do something. That certainly is one way of learning, but too long. Then they spend their remaining years in regret.

They can learn the right way or they can learn the long way. They can learn on purpose or they can learn by accident. It's a choice. How should they spend their time? As I said before, the clocks are ticking. There are no time outs.

Kids can learn by accident or they can learn on purpose. Whether by purposeful learning or by accidental learning, crisis is still needed to change the habit pattern. The difference is, accidental crisis creates problems. Purposeful crisis creates success.

Accidental crisis occurs like a pressure cooker exploding. When the new situation can't tolerate the old behavior any longer, you have a crisis that creates a change in a direction to solve the problem. Some families' bounce like a pinball from one problem to the next, but that isn't necessary. Purposeful learning first determines the desired direction, and then gradually creates the necessary crisis for change. This is what every good parent and boss should do. It's called "Holding the carrot out in front". Don't wait for bankruptcy to strike for change to happen.

Let's take a look at how crisis works to change habit patterns. An interesting habit pattern that I see two and three year old children acquire is to fall face down on the floor when they want something that has been denied or when they dislike something. They can do it quietly or they can do it with a whine and a cry. Children rarely do this in the privacy of their own rooms but almost always in the path most frequently traveled. The habit pattern is always successful. It gets parents' attention, forcing them to take action to focus on the child and give them whatever they need. That behavior is a habit pattern, a rather successful one, too. It gets children what they want. After all, if you could create a behavior that whenever you displayed it people would attend immediately to your needs, you would use it frequently too. People search all their lives to discover that habit pattern.

#5. CREATING CHANGE BY NOT FULFILLING NEEDS

Falling face down on the floor crying when kids want something is called a tantrum, but it is a habit pattern.

I asked one parent, "How do you think your child learned that kind of behavior?"

"I don't understand," she said.

"Your child had to learn it somehow. What do you think the cause was?"

After discussing the situation, the mother realized that even when her child was just one day old, whenever he would lay face down and cry, she would go over and check his needs. I've even seen some families arrange elaborate schedules just to fulfill this task. That's where habit patterns begin to form, and children learned these patterns because they were successful in helping them attain their basic needs to survive. Later you still find children practicing old habit patterns that proved quite effective even though they're not in the crib anymore. Even though the children can now communicate in other ways, they're still using old habit patterns.

Whenever children have tantrums, just ignore them. If they're in the way, as they often are, then take them to their room, nothing else. Don't reinforce the behavior by giving them the attention they want Parents and teachers often unknowingly reinforce the very behaviors they want to change by saying something, changing facial expressions to show annoyance, or even punishing the child.

To form positive habit patterns, teach children directly what they need to know to get what they want. Tell children how they are to react: "If you desire my attention, come over to me, touch my leg and say 'Mom, I need some help. '*' Or if the child hasn't learned to talk yet, teach the child an appropriate nonverbal behavior involving touching, or a simple request such as "Up!"

But words are not enough. Behavior is affected by action, not words. Actions speak louder than words. We must show children by actually modeling the desired behavior. It won't take longer than seven days to change that habit pattern if you're consistent with the consequences not fulfilling what they want. Every time you're inconsistent, just add another seven days for the behavior change. If you're not consistent, you'll spend ninety percent of your time nagging and ten percent enjoying the time with your kids. Remember, children obey for the same reason they break the rules: The rewards for doing the right action is more beneficial.

One ten months old boy changed the whining behavior to taking personal responsibility by crawling over to his mother, touching her finger and saying "Up!" with a smile. Seven days prior that same child was lying on the floor in the kitchen and crying. We created die crisis, the opportunity for change, by not fulfilling the needs.

What if you did nothing at all? Wouldn't the behavior just go away? Life doesn't work that way. Only those who do the work will get the pay.

The laws that govern nature and your personal life are not optional. You cannot break the laws you can only demonstrate them. If you fall off a building you are not breaking the law of gravity, you are demonstrating it. When the difference between what you have and what you want becomes great enough, you can either change your wants to match what you have, becoming unhappy and uninspired, or you can change what you're doing to get what you want, becoming happy and inspired.

Most parents choose to change the expectations they have for their children to match what they have, resulting with living uninspired and unhappy lives. Not because they want it that way-everybody wants to have what they want-they just don't know what to do. When a tantruming, moody child creates a crisis for the parents-what the parents want is to spend a quiet evening and what they have differs greatly-the parents usually choose to give the child what the child wants thinking that will also give them what they want. This remedy is only temporary, however, because they are strengthening the behaviors they don't want.

If parents want their kids to be successful, they must create the opportunity for crisis in much the same way as a good employer does for his workers-he doesn't demand a change, he inspires a change in effort and attitude.

A young married woman came to me concerning her husband's pouting behavior. Whenever he wanted attention he went into the doldrums. He'd go lie down on the couch in the middle of the family room, turn on the television and say, "I just don't have any energy. I don't feel well!"

She would walk up to him and say, "What's the matter? Can I help?"

"No. Nothing's wrong," he would reply.

"Are you sure?"

The husband would answer in a quiet, almost pouting voice, "Yes, I'm sure."

Remember Ryan's behavior of running through the house, slapping people on their backs yelling, "Sucker" when he wanted attention?

Where did the husband learn that habit pattern? It's probably left over from the crib. You can change that behavior by creating a crisis - not giving die husband what he wants.

The next time the husband pulled this behavior, his wife merely asked, "Is there anything the matter?" She had little sympathy in her voice, like she was asking directions from a stranger.

"No. I'm OK."

The wife asked once more for clarity, "Are you sure, honey? You look so sad."

"No, nothing at all," he replied, irritated. "Nothing, nothing."

The wife sighed with relief. "Well, I'm so glad there is nothing wrong. I was so afraid that you were in pain or something. Now I won't have to worry. If you would like to talk I'll be in the other room."

The husband went into absolute crisis. He didn't know what to do. He sat there for a little while, and then tried the old behavior again by moaning a little louder.   No response.

The next few times the behavior occurred, it was shorter and shorter until finally the husband learned that he could get a positive response by going to his wife and saying, "You know honey, I've been thinking about some things and I would like to sit down and talk with you about them. " He learned how to take responsible action. Of course this could be any age child. *We create change by not fulfilling the desire.*

Tina's mom called me again from Hawaii concerned now about her three-year-old boy's remission in toilet training. When he had to do something he didn't like, he would choose to dirty his pants when it bothered Mom the most either while shopping with mom or on social visits with the family. She reported that he wouldn't do it all at one time, but just a little each time for the desired effect. We merely had to change that unacceptable habit pattern by creating the crisis that would create an opportunity for change.

Mom created the crisis by explaining to her son that wetting pants was a young child's behavior and that young children don't have the same privileges as older children. Older children have the option of playing outside frequently, staying up late, choosing their snacks and television programs, and partaking in games with other children. These privileges are designed for older children who have accepted more personal responsibility, one of which is being responsible for their personal needs. She explained to him that if he chose not to be responsible for his personal needs that it was OK, but the action told her that he didn't have the responsibility of an older child. When he chose to take the responsibility of older kids, then he could do what older kids do. He will have earned privileges. Mom knew from working with his older sister Tina, regarding being responsible for cleaning her room, that behavior is affected by action, not words. She knew that he would test The System and that she would have to follow through.

Mom followed through on what she said. Whenever her son chose to have these remissions in toilet training, he wasn't able to play on the bikes with the other kids, stay up late with the other kids, but rather went to bed with the other little children. He was treated like a very young child, one that lacked responsibility. It created a crisis for the child because what the child wanted and what the child was getting weren't the same. The desires were not being fulfilled. The crisis forced the child to make the decision to be more responsible for his actions. He changed because it was entirely up to him to change.

In good business, a crisis always exists. Those who do the work get the pay. If workers want more, then they must choose to change old habit patterns for new ones that will allow them to achieve. As children learn to be responsible for their actions, they're learning how to achieve success.   They're learning how to get what they want by learning how to change.

Taking personal responsibility for their actions allow them to do just that. It is a learned behavior. They learn that they can't have more for doing what they do, they must learn how to do more to deserve more. Neither workers nor school children can expect to achieve without work. They must learn how to create the crisis by creating the desire that excites them to take action. They must learn how to be their own boss. The earlier in life they learn this part of the game of life, the sooner they will become successful, but until they learn how to be the boss, the parent needs to be the boss.

Without crisis there can be no change. A child will continue to tantrum. A mate will continue to pout.   A worker will complain about his lifestyle.

Crisis is important to move kids from one learned behavior to the next.

Parents must create the structure for change until children learn how to create the change to get what they want. Unfortunately most wait for crisis to force them out of old habit patterns. They live from problem to problem not from success to success.

My wonderful aunt on my father's side would have probably said,

"I've never heard such a crock. Say it simply. An ounce of prevention is worth a pound of cure." Most parents could benefit from my aunts advice. Teachers and parents often fail to recognize the minor problem until it turns into a crisis. They wait until the childish behavior outgrows its usefulness before taking action. Then they usually implement some form of major punishment. If that doesn't change the behavior, they try it again. They live in turmoil.

If you don't correct the minor problems, they will not go away- they will EXPLODE! You must create the situation that creates the opportunity for change until kids learn that they can take control. You create the crisis or you live with the problems. That is the game of life.

#6. SUCCESS TAKES PRACTICE

If children have the opportunity, they can become successful at most anything they want to do, but only if they are willing to work at it. Forming good habit patterns takes practice.

Practice makes perfect. If you want to become good at anything, you have to do it often. There's no substitute for practice. Whether you're talking about becoming a good student, a tennis player, riding a skateboard, or even being a good parent.

How long do you want it to take to become good at what you do? If you just do it once in a while if 11 take forever. To do it well is to do it often. It can't be perfected without experience. You've got to get out there and do it. There is no substitute for practice. Many fail because they're just not willing to do what it takes.

#7. KEEP IT SIMPLE

The sooner you help kids learn how to play the game of life, the sooner they can get on with getting what they want.   It may sound a little silly, almost too easy.   It is.

A single parent with three children told me that two of her children learned how to play the game. They learned that it was easier, faster, and more fun to be responsible for their actions. They do their work, get the grades, do their chores, get it over with and get on with the things they want to do. The older children figured it out, but her youngest still didn't get it.

He spent more time trying to get out of his responsibilities than it would have taken to complete them. He was making it complicated. He wasn't having any fun because he hadn't learned how to get what he wanted. Every second was a struggle. To him, life just wasn't simple. Some kids grow up never learning how the game of life operates and everything all the time seems like such a struggle.

Life wasn't designed to be complicated; people make it so. If it becomes complicated, then you're not doing something right. Keep it simple. Any other direction is just plain stupid because it simply doesn't work. Why do something that doesn't work?

#8. KIDS CAN CHANGE DIRECTION

Cause and effect puts everyone on a certain direction for a destination. A child's ultimate destination is adulthood. All of us hope that they'll be successful adults. They will surely arrive someday-the question is "Where do you want them to go?"

I spent the evening having dinner with some friends. After dinner, the kids were sent to bed and we stepped out on the patio to enjoy the evening.

Almost immediately their four-year-old daughter started to cry. My friend's wife asked him to go inside and check on her. When the host returned, he announced that their baby couldn't sleep because we were outside. My friends picked up their wine glasses and said, "Time for the baby to go to bed. She wants us inside now. "

We all shuffled into the house, immediately.

From the doorway, the child observed our obedience. The parents performed the duty as if it was as natural to the routine of parenthood as giving birth. These same parents continually remind others of the pain and frustration of parenthood.

I can hardly believe these parents like the situation, which brings up a curious point. Why do parents tolerate behavior from children they would never tolerate from anyone else? I believe they simply don't know what to do about it. Parents don't go around creating this kind of behavior intentionally. They usually make a lot of little turns in the wrong direction until gradually they wake up one morning and there stands the little tyrant. It happens so gradually that most parents presume the behavior is normal.

It doesn't have to be that way tomorrow. If you wake up some morning and say, "I don't want to be here!" you can change the direction. As long as you continue to breathe, you are in the game. The only thing you can't do is stop the clock.

Determining direction and destination is merely an honest answer to a simple question: "Are you satisfied with where you are right now?" If not, then change direction. If you are, then do more of what you're already doing. The game of life isn't complicated; it's fun.

There is no mystery surrounding raising successful, happy kids. Raising kids for success is playing the game according to the law. How the game turns out is left strictly up to you. Why do some win better than others? They know how to play. And it doesn't matter what they are doing now or what you have done in the past. Forget the past, it's merely playing the game, doing things a certain way, everyday, step by step. That's all there is to it. If you follow the steps you'll get what you want. There is no reason why you shouldn't become really successful in developing success-oriented kids. Good cause, good effect. Living each day successfully will have an accumulative effect for the good.

The System works. Make it work for you by creating opportunities for change.

5

The System At Home

Here's The System I use in my classroom and in my home to help kids be successful and happy. It incorporates the laws of behavior and the laws of success. It's the same system they'll be asked to participate in as adults in the work force. You can use The System in your home too, to create positive changes in your kids.

The System contains daily routines that I use in my classroom, routines that impose the structure of self-responsibility. These are the same kinds of structures that you use to be a successful adult and will probably be required of your kids as they enter the real world of work. Adapting these structures to your home will help your children to succeed even faster. It allows them to enjoy childhood and grow up with complete freedom because the structure allows them to be in complete control. They'll have learned the necessary routines for success, which will allow them to get on with the more important activities of growing up and living.

With The System, you're literally teaching your kids how to win. They were born with this ability, but they have to be taught the rules - then they'll know how to achieve anything they want. Through routine and structure in their daily work, you will teach them through action how to win.

Who does the managing in The System? Initially I do in the classroom and you do at home. After twenty-one days, however, the kids will begin to manage themselves because they know that by following The System, they'll achieve and get what they want After all, that's the whole secret. Everybody wants to have what they want.

Basically, The System has six simple steps:

#1. Attitude

#2. Establish Expectations and Privileges

#3. Establish Zones of Appropriate Behavior

#4. Model Appropriate Behaviors

#5. Design a Daily Duty Roster

#6. Write a mutually agreed upon Contract with your children. That's all there is to it.

#1. ATTITUDE: SETTING THE ATMOSPHERE FOR SUCCESS

In my classroom hangs a large sign that reads:

RED HOT AND ROLLING!

Each and every morning when my kids come into the classroom I ask them, "How do you feel today?" In unison they yell, "Red hot and rolling!!!"

I control the attitude in my classroom, initially. Later on when the kids have learned how to achieve, they control their attitude.

If I have a good attitude when I come to work I'm going to achieve much better. And the people I'm going to be around are going to achieve. Watch the people at work who are achieving. Check their attitude. Achieving in any field requires a positive attitude of expectancy. The same thing applies with the kids. Attitude is 90 percent of the game, so when their attitude is right, they're 90 percent already there.

How do you want your kids to feel at home? Red hot and rolling! How do you want them to feel out there in the work force? Red hot and rolling! People with the positive red hot and rolling attitudes are the kinds of people other people want to be around. It's interesting that the kids who have a better attitude always achieve more pay, complete work faster, and always enjoy their privilege time.   Is it really any different in the real work world?

Check out your own attitude toward your kids, too. Before your kids can become the people you want them to be, you must first imagine them as the kind of people you want them to be. You cannot create what you cannot imagine. You must change your attitude toward your kids before your kids can change.

If your child comes home late from school every day and you don't like it, check your own attitude. Do you say, "Hey you little bonehead, I told you to be home on time. You're late!" Or, do you say, "You're getting home earlier and earlier. It's good to have you home. " Their tardy action may not earn them a reward, but a token step in the right direction deserves an encouraging word. Your words should always guide your kids in the direction you want them to be going.

Kids need to learn that it's their attitude toward the situation that counts and it's not the situation that determines their attitude. They learn it now, or they learn it tomorrow. If they get their attitude right, they can have anything they want in this world.

#2. PRIVILEGES AND EXPECTATIONS: LEARNING TO EARN REWARDS PRIVILEGES

First, we need to make a list of your child's Privileges. Since children's behavior is learned on the basis of how their rewards are earned, it's important to establish at the onset exactly what will motivate your child to change.

Why do we use Privileges instead of punishment? Punishment requires mat the parent take responsibility. The parent shouldn't be taking responsibility, the child should. How do you get children to take responsibility? How do you get anyone to take responsibility? This is one of the major questions of parents, teachers, employers and spouses. How do you motivate people to want to take responsibility?

The answer is to use the same rules in the home that are used in business. When you take responsibility at work and do your job, you get a reward: your paycheck. When kids take responsibility and do their kid jobs (schoolwork, chores around the house), they get a reward. What do you reward them with? Privileges that they enjoy and probably take for granted.

So write out the official Privilege list. Jot down all of your children's current Privileges, then prioritize them with number one being the Privilege most enjoyed. Watching television is always up there at the top of the list as well as playing with friends after school. For younger kids, it's socializing. For older kids it's usually driving the car and weekly allowance. That's their pay for doing their kid jobs. Those who do the work get the pay and those who don't do the work don't get the pay. It's that simple.

When I first go into the home, I find out immediately what a child's paycheck is, what their Privileges are. Every human being has a pay system. Every cat, every dog, every five-month old child and every adult has a pay system that motivates them to act in a certain way, at a specific time and place. We all work for rewards and recognition.

"What is their pay?" I ask parents.

"What do you mean? They don't get paid," they'll often reply.

For so long the unspoken agreement between parent and child has been, "Mom and Dad will do everything and the kids will do nothing and receive everything unless they cause Mom and Dad major discomfort". That's the usual situation. Who is ultimately in control of the consequences? Neither parry. Not a fun relationship.

Once the parents understand the payoff system, they'll usually answer, "Well, he likes to ride his bike, he likes to go out with his friends as soon as he gets home from school, he likes to watch television after dinner, but especially on Saturday mornings. On the weekends he likes to go fishing with his father. He likes to help me make dinner, especially desserts. He likes special treats on Friday night when his friends come over. " All those are pay, his Privileges. Privileges are not something really special kids receive beyond their daily pay if they act a certain way, which would be an artificial system that does not exist in the real work world. The enjoyment of daily Privileges is the action of fulfilling defined Expectations. Privileges are their pay for learning how to be responsible people.

EXPECTATIONS

Next, make a list of Expectations. The Expectations for kids should always be the same and should always be posted. Notice I don't call them laws or rules. These are the Expectations a child must accomplish in order to get what they want. Keep it simple. There are five Expectations in my classroom:

*Always do your best work.

*Listen when the teacher or other adult is talking.

*Raise your hand if you have something to ask, and then wait to be called on.

*Get along with other children.

*Work quietly and complete assignments on time.

Notice within these five Expectations is built-in achievement. They are all expressed in positive language and involve positive behaviors. These five Expectations could probably apply to your home as well as most jobs. If children are following each Expectation, excellence in learning and behavior will be achieved.

In the classroom, I always keep the Expectations posted in the front of the room. They are as visible as the posted expectations on the highways. If the signs aren't visible, then you're not communicating the Expectations.

Highway signs are posted all the time to allow you to be responsible for your actions. If you're ticketed for inappropriate driving behaviors and you go to court, they'll ask you if you saw the posted signs. The same procedure works in my classroom and in your home. It doesn't change.

In your home the Expectations should be posted where the entire family can see them. It works well to post one copy on the refrigerator and another in the child's bedroom. Make it easy to read and fun to look at.

Your Expectations at home will be slightly different than the ones

I use in my classroom. A family in Hawaii has these Expectations posted on their refrigerator:

*Be courteous.

*Have a positive attitude.

*Complete all homework.

*Treat the belonging of others with care.

*Complete chores cheerfully and efficiently.

*Obey requests.

Make a separate piece of paper with each child's name listed on it. Whenever a child isn't following the Expectations, put a check by his or her name. Ten checks means the child hasn't earned their Privileges. When it's time for the Privileges (watching television or whatever), just say; "Take a look at the Expectations. If you have ten checks after your name, you have chosen not to participate in the Privileges. " The child continues working or otherwise keeping occupied without the Privileges. Twice a day the kids have an opportunity to start with a new chart.

Now comes the bonus. In my classroom I have what I call the Privilege Paycheck. You'll see how I use it in a later section, but here's how it works. Save all the checkmark charts during the week and on Friday issue the Privilege Paycheck. It can be real allowance or imaginary money redeemable for special privileges. You can use any amount of money; in my classroom I use five dollars. Each checkmark during the week subtracts five cents from the Paycheck. Children may earn as little as eighty cents, or the full five dollars.   You can adjust the monetary values, as needed depending on the age and needs of the child.

Having Expectations allows you to check on children's behaviors. They allow you to guide your children instead of judging them. There is no emotion and therefore no stress.

Without expectations you can't check behavior because there's nothing to check against. It would be like flying in an airplane whose pilot didn't have a destination, just flying in any direction until it ran out of gas. When you have the written expectations, you have a destination.

RESPONSIBILITY IS FULFILLING EXPECTATIONS TO GET

PRIVILEGES

Children learn to be responsible by earning their Privileges through fulfilling their Expectations. In my classroom, every time the Expectations are followed the children earn their Privileges. Whenever an Expectation isn't followed the children get a check by their name and don't earn their Privileges. When it's time for a Privilege I merely say, 'Take a look at the Expectations. Children who have checks after their names have chosen not to participate in their Privilege but have chosen to continue working. The rest of you may enjoy yourselves. "

Twice a day they have an opportunity to start with a new chart. I save the old charts with checks to help determine their earned bonus on Friday. For adults at work the earned privilege is called a break. If you do your work according to expectations, you can have the privilege. If you don't meet expectations you lose the privilege. The same thing applies with the kids.

Kids know The System works, but they'll test it for its consistency and honesty. If children choose to stay after school to complete their work rather than doing it in school, then they will arrive home late and are choosing not to participate in one of their Privileges like watching television or playing with friends. The next day they are welcome to earn those Privileges again.

After about three weeks the parents are delighted. There is less yelling and screaming, and the kids gradually become responsible for their actions. They learn that it's easier to get the work done when it needs to be done because then they are able to get what they want when they want it. Isn't that what everyone wants?

It's important to teach through structure rather than merely communicate what needs to be done. Why? Because the system works on action. Have you ever merely called the electric company and communicated that the check was in the mail? You know the answer. The real system works through attitude and rewards, which are really just action steps in the direction of getting what you want. Communication is less effective. That parents, teachers, and employers define, monitor, and reward the behavior of an individual in a routine and structured manner is crucial if they are going to be effective in getting the job done responsibly.

With clear Expectations and Privileges, kids can control their consequences 100 percent. They have 100 percent freedom to express themselves in their environment. They know the extension of their behavior all the time. They're in control.

THE BEHAVIOR RULE OF THUMB

One problem that comes up for parents is distinguishing between their child's need for expression and inappropriate behavior. They don't want to stifle any creative growth. Maybe your kids are constantly interrupting your telephone conversations with something exciting to share but you think, 'I hate to tell them to wait. They look so excited.' When the family decides to take a bike ride to the park and one child says they don't want to go, is that OK? Is that a successful behavior for work? Is that really a bad attitude? There are many pestering questions of indecision.

To a child, the need for attention is everything. If you could penetrate a child's inner thoughts, you could hear a savage screaming, "I want! I want! I want!" It's an impulse for immediate satisfaction. They never get enough, and their reach for more will stretch beyond your grasp in to new frontiers where all children dare to go.

A child's failure to meet expectations isn't blatant, it's very subtle. It's these subtle areas where the headaches begin and a system begins to break down. Why should your child be so subtle? If kids can get attention without fulfilling expectations, then why achieve? I call this area the grey frontier-a place of seemingly boundless space, no right or no wrong.

Characteristics of the grey frontier are most important to identify/ but most difficult because you're conditioned to them. You've existed in the midst of them for so long that you have become insensitive. It's like having lived at the base of a mountain for so long that you cease to even see it. Grey frontiers are as subtle as the way you talk. This difficulty creates confusing problems for parents because when their children reach into the grey frontier, they usually don't know how to react.

A while back I was visiting a friend who happens to be a psychologist, and a very good one I should note. Some other couples were visiting and talking on various topics. They all appeared to be having a good time. His four children were entertaining themselves.

Suddenly, the host's 13-year-old son became quite upset about his younger sister playing with the train set. She had derailed a few cars and dismantled some track while he was gone. The son was fit to be tied. His father discovered that the incident described had taken place two weeks before.

The host went inside the house to see his son. About a half hour later, he returned. He was concerned and a little embarrassed, "His being upset is logical, but why does he choose to get upset now, in the midst of all the guests?" A father concerned and a party disturbed by the grey frontier.

I don't have to go through a lot of analysis trying to determine which behaviors are good, which behaviors are bad, which behaviors warrant special attention and which do not. I give parents one simple rule that I've learned to use every day in the classroom and in the home. Without it I think I'd go crazy.

Here's my Behavior Rule of Thumb:

If all the kids were to have the same behavior, at the same time and at the same place every day, would it be OK?

If the answer is "No!" then that behavior is inappropriate for that time and place.

Would it be OK for all the children all the time to interrupt your telephone conversations? No. If in the middle of dinner one of your children suddenly says, "Can I have my dessert? Would it be OK?" Maybe you might think that he's cleaned his plate, or maybe this one time he could have dessert in the middle of his dinner? That child has interrupted the entire dinner. Just ask yourself, 'If all the kids in the neighborhood were at this dinner table every night saying at the same time, "Can I have my dessert?' Would it be OK?" Would you be running a dinner that would be pleasant and sociable for everyone?' If you cannot answer yes, then the behavior is inappropriate.

STARTING THEM EARLY

You can expect your children to be responsible for their behavior when they are as young as twenty-one days. The first twenty-one days should be spent acclimating to their new environment but after that, they can be responsible.

The problem with very young children is not their lack of ability to be responsible, but their limited ability to express their needs. Very young children communicate primarily through crying, whining and yelling. Their needs are very basic. Are they hungry? Do they need to be changed? Are they free from pain? Check to see if all their basic needs have been met, then apply the Behavior Rule of Thumb: If all the children were to have the exact same behavior, at the same time, at the same place, every day, would it be OK? If your answer is no, then that behavior is antisocial.

Once again we need to remember that the behavior itself isn't bad, the child just needs to learn that it's not appropriate for that particular time. After you've checked to make sure all their basic needs are met, if the baby is displaying inappropriate behavior you merely pick them up with a warm hug and put them in their playpen or nursery, isolated from the group and attention. Just leave them there until they have been playing quietly for ten minutes.

At home with my 18-month-old boy Michael, I use the kitchen stove clock with the buzzer for cooking as a timer. It's more for me than for Michael because it lets me know when it's time to go check. I set it for ten minutes and when the bell rings I walk to the door and listen. If he's playing quietly, I walk in, pick him up, bring him out to where we are and it all begins again like nothing happened. The results? We have fun enjoying each other's company.

Some parents ask me, "Well, what if you have a child that just refuses?"

That behavior will happen only once, if at all, when children are testing the system to get what they want. If that behavior does occur, you must physically pick the child up and remove him to where he needs to be: in his room, in the corner, in the crib. If it occurs again, gently slap his hand and remove him again. You must be firm, unemotional, and consistent. Be prepared for a lengthy dramatic tantrum, which you can just ignore. When he has displayed the proper behavior for ten minutes, then welcome him to return. You should only say, "Show me by your actions when you want your ten minutes to begin." Refusing to cooperate is a sign that too many minor problems are being overlooked and they need to be addressed.

The equation of Expectations and Privileges works in the real world of work. It might as well work in your home, too. It's the same system they will be responsible to as adults. The sooner they learn it, the happier they'll be. When the Expectations and consequences are clearly defined and adhered to, you'll have a blueprint for success.

#3. ZONES OF BEHAVIOR: LEARNING APPROPRIATE BEHAVIORS

One of the Expectations you'll probably have is for your child to behave appropriately in given situations. What does this really mean? Well, if you think about it, the behaviors themselves aren't bad, what makes them seem bad is that they get displayed in the wrong place, at the wrong time. It's not a behavioral problem; it's a *zone* problem.

My classroom is divided into three zones of behavior: The Work Zone, the Fun Zone, and the Silent Zone.

The work zone is where the kids work. What type of behavior do they have in this area? Work behaviors. Work behaviors are defined by the Expectations. When they are in the Work Zone, no one else exists in the room except the child, his work, and his desk.

At the right side of the room is the Fun Zone. Within this area is the freedom of kid behavior. Kid behavior is talking to each other, laughing, and playing the assorted games in the area, talking about the books and toys they may have shared that day with one another, and doing whatever kids do. That's their zone to do whatever they particularly want to do, if they have earned that privilege. Fun Zone behavior cannot disturb those in the Work Zone. Fun Zone behaviors are defined by the Expectations.

The back of the room is the Silent Zone. If for any reason a child receives three consecutive warnings in a three-minute period, then his behavior is depriving other students as well as himself the opportunity to achieve. At that point I ask the student to please take his work and move behind the partition. This child has chosen to work in the back of the room isolated from the rest of the class. In order to leave the Silent Zone a child must be working for ten consecutive minutes within the behaviors defined by the Expectations. After ten minutes the child has earned the Privilege to work with the rest of his classmates, at his own desk.

You may wonder, "Well, what if the student chooses not to work while behind the partition?"

All the children know that all time spent in the Silent Zone, excluding the ten consecutive working minutes, they owe to themselves at the end of the workday. While they are there, they have chosen not to participate in class activities. They belong to a separate class. They don't earn Privileges or get warnings.   If the class happens to be going out to recess, seeing a film, going on a field trip in the next few minutes, whatever we happen to be doing when they're back there, they don't belong. They have chosen not to belong. Will their work be accomplished? Of course. When? When they choose to accomplish it. Not when Mom, not when the teacher, and certainly not when the school district chooses-but-when the *child chooses* to have it accomplished.

How long are children usually behind the partition? Younger children five and under are usually there about five minutes, older children about ten to thirty minutes maximum. Children are behind the partition and are choosing not to complete their work because they're testing The System. Behavior is affected by action, not words. They're not willing to learn the new skills of attitude and rewards to acquire their wants if they can still use their infant learned skills of whining and yelling. They want the rewards and recognition like any of us, but they don't want to be responsible for their actions, especially if The System will yield to their demands. Once they recognize The System is consistent and honest-they always get the pay if they always do the work-they will have learned that it is easier to change to get what they want than it is to not get what they want. Kids are pretty smart.

Why all the different zones? Is it any different than what your kids are asked to adapt to when they graduate into the real world of work? They have the Work Zone at their place of employment, the Fun Zone when they are socializing with their friends or enjoying time at home, and the Silent Zone if they choose to disobey civil laws and are sent to jail. They're going to have these zones of behavior all their lives. Why not find out now that by acting appropriately in these zones of behavior, they can better achieve to get the things they want, whether it's a work behavior with their boss, or a relationship behavior with their friends.

Zones of behavior work in the classroom, in the real world, and also in the home.

Parents come to me all the time and say they wished their homes had the same zones of behavior that my classroom has. Then maybe they could have some peace and quiet. They always look astonished when I tell them that their homes have the same zones.   Your home does, too.

Get out a piece of paper and a pencil. Draw a floor plan picture of your home. Lets take the living room first. What kinds of behaviors belong in your living room? Write them down on another piece of paper under the room heading. Would you like your children to be congenial and quiet in the living room? How many living rooms are like that? Why aren't they? You really only need to define the zones and the behaviors in the zones to make them happen. There should be a whole list of behaviors, appropriate for each room. Define them just like a boss does at work, then follow through.

Why do the zones of behavior work? Consistency is a key within any business or home. It's hard to deny the honesty and the consistency of a system that rewards right action.

What happens when an adult displays inappropriate behavior in the work area? They're isolated. It's called suspension without pay. After a certain amount of time, usually ten days, they're allowed to return. I put my 18 month old son Michael in his room for ten minutes. When he's playing comfortably he's welcome to return. When someone in the work force displays appropriate behavior they're welcome to come back. The difference between child and adult is that a person in the work force who doesn't conform within a specified period is asked to leave. Their boss doesn't have the love and patience of a parent. The zones of behavior were not created by me; it's a system that exists. You can use it to win or not use it and lose. Your children can learn appropriate behaviors that apply everywhere they go if you create the opportunity by creating the structure in your home.

TAKING RESPONSIBILITY FOR PERSONAL BELONGINGS

One of the primary zone problems in most homes is caring for personal belongings. The problem is not that kids have belongings, it's that they need to keep them in the right zone. Here's how I handle this zone problem in my classroom.

Kid's bring all kinds of personal belongings to school: beeping watches, combs, brushes, pens, fancy pencils, erasers, bracelets, toys, and many other things that have the potential of distracting them from their goal of achieving their work.

If these items become a distraction while they're in the Work Zone, it becomes a violation of the fifth Expectation (working quietly and doing their best work). When this occurs, I simply take the item away and put it in the Classroom Store. For example, if during class their watch begins to beep because they set an alarm that distracts other kids' attention, or they're playing with bracelets when they should be working, into the Classroom Store it goes.

The items that I take are wrapped with a piece of paper, marked with their name and a dollar value. Each week when the store opens, they have the opportunity to purchase it back with their Privilege Paycheck. That's their choice if they choose to bring it to class. If they choose to bring it, and it distracts them from their work and distracts other students, then the entire system becomes more stressful. If it was a place of business, the same distracting behaviors would cut down on productivity and the overall ramifications would probably be a loss of privileges.

It's the same as if you choose to park your car in a No Parking zone for your own convenience and pleasure, but at the inconvenience of others. If you choose to do that, the city says, "It's OK with us. " They merely tow it away to the impounding area and if you want it back, you go to work, you earn your paycheck, and you give them a portion of your hard earned dollars to get back your car. The longer it's impounded, the more of your dollars you have to pay.   Does the system work? Yes!

I used to be notorious for always trying to find a quick and easy way to park my car. After all, I wasn't going to pay some joker $7.00 just to park my car. I thought the fee was outrageous until one midnight when my wife and I came out of the theatre to find our car missing. We had to take a taxi home. The next morning was Easter Sunday. I had to wake up early and take a taxi to the impounding garage and pay $55.00 to get my car back. The people at the garage weren't even sympathetic. The entire fiasco cost me about $85.00. Did the city yell at me for this behavior? No. They didn't care how I wanted to spend my money. What if I didn't have any money for the taxi or the impounding garage? I think you know the answer to that. Now I always park in the designated areas. If I'm in a hurry, I pay a parking garage their meager amount for the convenience.   Did I curse the system? No.   I was upset with myself. I vowed never to do that again. I've learned that this newly formed behavior of mine actually leaves me more time to do the things I really want to do.

Is it any different for the kids? No. It's the same system. They know it. That's why The System works. It's an honest system. If the attitude is right and the rewards are there and they're consistent, then The System builds success within the individual. If they form the right attitudes for the right rewards, they win. Who's in control? They are, and they know it. That's why it works so well. How do you develop routines for taking responsibility for personal belongings in the home? I've visited homes that when I walked into the living room I could barely find a path to walk or a place to sit because of all the toys strewn around. This isn't an unusual experience. The parents usually run about like little servants picking them up, apologizing for the mess and behavior saying, "It's so difficult to keep up. The kids start playing and then they just forget to put them away. " I usually have to move a doll or a jeep from the chair before sitting.

Are the kids concerned? No. Why should they be? They're happy as the Rockefellers sleeping in their cozy beds while the servants clean. The parents usually comment that it's become such a constant battle, but they figure the children will learn someday.   There is a way to change this behavior, if you want to teach your child responsibility for what they'll be responsible for later.

Have you ever been upset with your roommate or your spouse who doesn't put things back where they belong after using them? I've seen relationships ruined because of that kind of behavior. My wife and I used to get like fighting dogs and pouting children over that behavior. Oh, the time wasted on such things when we could have been living and experiencing the excitement of each other's company. There are a lot of lawyers out there willing to help out such ailing relationships.

The simple solution was just sitting down and talking about the different zones of behavior that each of us appreciates. We came to one impasse: she didn't like ironing my clothes, frankly because she hated ironing. Solution? Either I learn to like ironing or I send it out to be done, getting back to dipping into the paycheck routine. The other option would be to wear wrinkled clothes. Whose fault would that be? Mine.   Who do I blame? Me.

I hate clothes strewn about. I'm a neatness nut. My wife is just the opposite. The solution was for my wife to pick up her things and put them where they belong or I toss everything of hers into the wash regardless of its care requirements. Back into the pocketbook and dwindling results.

We solved the problem without a lawyer. We merely sat down and designed our own agreement for happiness. It read, "If we want to be happy then we must do this... If we don't want to be happy then we can do this... "Of course, we could have had five frustrating years of wasted company and then paid a lawyer to contract our differences. I know it sounds comical/ but those situations happen every day.

If you want your kids to take better care of their belongings, it's very simple. First, you sit down and draw out a floor plan determining the zones of behavior and current privileges. Decide whether their toys need to be in the Play Zones like their bedroom or the back yard, and where they need to be at the end of the day.

If for some reason the children choose to leave their toys out or in the wrong zone, then they choose not to have those toys and must use some Privilege, which is really their pay, to get them back. If they choose not to use their Privileges or part of their allowance to purchase their toy, then the toy is sold at auction to the other children, just like the car that has been impounded. The parent can offer it to another sibling or take the child to some needy organization and donate the toy to children who will really appreciate the privilege of playing with it. It's important for parents to take their children with them to show them where the toy is going and let them know it's their choice.

How many times does this happen? Once! That's all. How many times did I have to take a taxi to the impounding area to get my car on my day off? Once! How many times did I wear a wrinkled shirt in the morning when I didn't take the time to iron? Once! How many times do the kids at school have to buy back their own toys or watch some other children purchase them while they're testing the consistency of the system? Once!

The System works. It all depends on their choices. You can offer the same choices to your kids. When the consequences are consistent and The System is honest - kids are in control of their rewards they learn that to be responsible for their actions gets them what they want. When kids reach that stage of development, they become dynamic, well adjusted kids. The System builds success within the individual.

#4. MODELING: TEACHING KIDS DIRECTLY WHAT WE WANT THEM TO LEARN

When I sit down with children on the first day of school or if I am working with them in their home, I model each and every expectation. I tell them and show them and then have them tell me and show me. It's just like a mirror- I have them mirror back the expectation, then there is no doubt in their minds what they need to do in order to achieve.

If you want a specific behavior, if you want someone to do something specifically, then you show them how to do it. That's all. Very simple. I call that Modeling The Behavior.

If I tell kids I want them to be working quietly and doing their best work, I actually sit down in the chair and show them how to work quietly and do their best work: sitting in their chair with their feet under the desk, papers out on top of the desk, working on a specific assignment that's defined for them on the board, and how to move on to another piece of work and get help if they're having problems. I even accidentally break one of my pencils and model how to put it inside the desk and retrieve the sharpened pencil and then continue. They are shown exactly how it is to be done. I also model how it's not to be done. One behavior fulfills the expectations while the other does not. One behavior learns to pay and the other does not. If they fulfill the expectations they get the love recognition that the behavior deserves. They are rewarded with the Privileges and the warm smiles that say, 'Job well done.   You're special!"

Show them exactly what they need to do in order to achieve. Take playing with toys, for example. Model where to play with the toys, how to play with them and where and how to put their toys away. Show them specifically - get down on the floor and play with them.

Maybe you want to teach them a bedtime routine, able manners, or even how to play with other children. If you're defining areas of behavior in your home, then you should define them for each area, both the right way and the wrong way. Model the playtime behaviors in the acceptable play areas and the exact same behaviors in the unacceptable areas like the living room and dining area. Show them specifically what's expected in order to earn the recognition and Privileges.

If you start a new job, you don't know how to do something and you get chewed out for doing it wrong, whose fault is it? You displayed a behavior that didn't match the expected expectations. The behavior isn't wrong. It's not your fault. There's nothing wrong with the behavior, it just didn't belong at a certain time and a certain place. Whose fault? It's the fault of whoever has failed to model for you exactly what they want. When they model the behaviors, then you can succeed and be responsible. If children get yelled at for sitting with their feet on the furniture and you tell them to sit correctly, but have never modeled sitting correctly, you're going to have frustrated children. The end result is called parent burnout.

An eight-year-old child brought to school his parents' adult magazine. The administration was in an uproar. I've never seen such a display of recognition for this child. Administration insisted that the child be severely punished and asked me to suggest an appropriate punishment.

"Have you ever told this student or any other student that these kinds of magazines may be appropriate for some parents who choose to have them, but they aren't appropriate for school?" I asked.

"'That's ridiculous/' the administrator replied. "Some things they're just supposed to know. Do we have to tell them every little thing?"

"No," I said. "Only the things we expect of them. Why do we educate them as to the dangers of drugs?"

The administrator thought I was taking this just a little too far and suspended the child from school. When the kid returned, he had an I-don't-care attitude. The administration called it a bad attitude problem. I think he was frustrated with a system that lacked consistency and honesty. If that same child was in a work situation, he'd probably quit, and I'm sure that his employer would find few dependable employees until he changed his training policy.

When you model exactly what needs to be done, tasks are completed. Giving your children feedback- "Hey, you're doing great!"- allows you to immediately correct your child's movements, to get them back on track, and to do what they need to do in order to reach your expectation. This gradually teaches them how to personally take responsibility for their own actions and how to achieve positive attention and privileges. Eventually you're going to be phased out, the teacher will be phased out, and your kids will be on their own-happy, successful, and knowing how to perform productive behaviors.

#5. THE DAILY DUTY ROSTER: TELLING KIDS WHAT THEY NEED TO DO

Hanging directly in front of my classroom is a monitor chart. It's similar to a roster. A daily duty is pinned next to each name. Every evening a pinned duty is moved down, assigning a student a different duty for each day.

Each child has a duty for the day. The first two days of school, each duty is modeled. For example, the door person is shown how to answer the door as described and how not to answer the door. I model to the rest of the class how they are supposed to stay on task while duties are performed. They are not even supposed to raise their heads at the sound of someone knocking at the door. Both the correct way and the incorrect way are modeled.

Each morning the students' names and their daily duties read: 'Tommy, you're door person today. Mark, you'll water the plants if they need it. Mary, you've got Mr. B. duty today, so you'll help me out around the classroom. Bonnie..." Their duties change daily. Every student knows exactly what they need to do each and every day. Even if they want to look up in advance to see what they would be doing the next day or even a week from now, all they have to do is look at the chart.

Do they have to ask me, "What do I have to do today?" No. They control their actions. They merely look up at the chart and schedule their time and activity.

Do you have a daily roster on your refrigerator at home with all the different chores for each day of the week? Remember, chores are different than children's personal responsibilities like picking up their toys, making the beds, cleaning their room, putting their dirty clothes where they belong. Chores are jobs that need to be completed to insure the household operating, like mowing the lawn, taking out the trash, sweeping the walks, cleaning the garage, washing the dishes, pulling the weeds, bringing in the groceries, washing the car, cleaning the bathroom, folding the wash.

Do you have a list of duties at work? Of course you do. You have to, that's how jobs get done. You can't go to work and accomplish successfully whatever needs to be done without knowing what needs to be done. You can't very well become responsible for your own action if you don't know what's required of you. This is the major problem between kids and parents.

A good definition of a behavior problem is when one individual is creating a behavior that another individual doesn't want at a particular time. Children don't want to be a behavior problem any more than an adult would. Everybody wants to do the right thing. They want to be recognized. If they don't know what to do at any particular time, then they fill in with their own activities, and their activities may not be the activities you want. You must define for them what they need to do in order to be recognized. Everybody wants to be recognized. At work you want to be recognized as a good employee, as people who are doing their jobs well. You want to be recognized for what you do. You want to be recognized as good teachers and as good parents. Just recognized. It's the same with kids-they want to be recognized, too.

How do you teach kids how to get love and recognition from their fellow human beings? You do it by defining the duties that are required each and every day in order for them to succeed. As kids get older the duties don't need to be outlined on a day-to-day basis, they can think in longer terms. What must they do for an entire week, for a month? But initially, you must break those steps down daily in a roster chart to help kids achieve. Gradually, they'll be able to schedule their own duties in order to achieve. It's important to schedule a small number of duties at first. It's like the old riddle, "How do you eat an elephant? Bite by bite." How do you teach kids to be responsible adults? Bite by bite. How do you teach them to get the recognition they need to feel successful and to move on daily? Bite by bite. How are you going to learn as parents to get things done? Bite by bite. Some parents, however, think they can get away with throwing a huge elephant to their kids and saying, "Here! Eat it!" Kids get overwhelmed, and when kids are overwhelmed they get frustrated and don't know what to do. When they don't know what to do, they begin to fill in the activities with their own behaviors, and frequently those are not the behaviors that Mom and Dad want. So what do you have? A conflict between parents and children that just simply isn't any fun.

You must define the exact duties to be performed to get what you want. Once you do, your children will learn that they need to do these duties to get what they want. Pretty soon they learn, "Wow. If I do this, I'm able to get this." It's the same exciting system they're going to have when they're adults. If they learn it now, you're going to have some fantastic kids out there in the work force.

There's one final very important thing to remember about daily duties: acknowledge your child for a job well done. Thank them and praise them, let them know you appreciate their help and that this behavior has been noticed. Otherwise, you guessed it; they'll try to get your attention through misbehaving. A hug and a "thank you" are two of the best rewards a child can get.

#6. THE CONTRACT: WRITING AN AGREEMENT BETWEEN PARENT AND CHILD

What makes The System really work is a written contract that says, "When you're doing what needs to be done, when it needs to be done and where it needs to be done, you receive the rewards." It's a clear agreement between both parent and child of the defined expectations and consequences.

Kids need you to teach them directly. They shouldn't have to learn by accident. Don't leave success to chance. Kids need a better commitment to success. *If you want to get it right, you've got to write it down.*

If you want to be successful, take what's in your head and put it on paper, then operate from the paper. Before you can build anything, from a new house to new behaviors, you must be able to see the concrete plan. If you're building a house you determine all the things you like and don't like, assemble a drawing, men work from the drawing. Building a future for your children is far more important than building a house. If you want to be successful, then you must operate from a blueprint. Most parents leave it to chance and then become greatly disappointed at the results.

With written contracts, business people don't have to worry; they let the contract do the worrying. A contract is simply a voluntary agreement of consistency with defined consequences. Be consistent with the contract and reap rewards. Fail and reap the penalty. Operate from a blueprint. Why take chances?

Good business people always use written contracts as blueprints. They never operate from their head, always from the paper. All relationships are governed by written, verbal, or even unstated subconscious agreements. The more clearly these agreements are defined, the better the relationship. Everybody likes to know where they stand. Kids aren't any different.

When Mom first called me about her eight-year-old boy Don, she was rather frustrated. Don, up until then, had always cleaned his room. He never really made much of a fuss about it. In the past, if he refused to clean up, Mom would help him. This usually solved the problem. Lately, however, Don literally refused to clean his room. She mentioned that the dirty room wasn't really her concern, but rather his refusal to cooperate. His negative behavior concerning his bedroom was beginning to affect other areas of their family life. (A little nuisance never goes away. It just grows up into a monster - I'm referring to the behavior, not the child).

She tried every possible persuasion she could think of from special desserts, going to the movies, and even new toys. Finally, she screamed out the penalty, "I'll trash all your toys!"

"You trash my toys and I'll run away and never talk to you again!" Don screamed back in reply.

The real reason Mom had called me was that she was afraid that Don would run away. She was afraid that perhaps she was demanding too much from her son and now she had lost him.

"Your fears are only fears," I said. "Your problem is not that you're demanding too much, but you're not demanding enough."
Mom didn't understand.

"You know what effect not cleaning his room has. His current behavior has promised you to design all your activities and thoughts around him. You're even calling long distance while Don is watching television. You're rewarding undeserved behavior, which always results in defiance because the child has no control. I think his actions are creating quite a disruptive effect on you, with really very few consequences for him."

Since she owned a small business, I asked her if her employees had any duties to perform at work. She laughed saying, "Yes. They're supposed to arrive at a certain time, complete defined tasks, and depart at a certain time. If all the tasks are not complete, they'll usually remain a little longer than usual to complete them. They're very responsible but I pay them well."

"And what is the effect of their actions?" I asked.

"A paycheck. Also, if any of my employees have any concerns about their jobs, they're welcome to discuss them with me at any time."

"It sounds like a good place to work," I said. "But what if an employee decides not to perform the defined duties? Are there any consequences?"

"An employee only receives pay for the work performed. Their situation is really no different from my own. If I don't do the work, I don't get paid."

"Have you ever become confused or irritated about this kind of cause and effect," I asked.

"No," she replied. "And if an employee chooses not to do the work for the pay that's their business, but that kind of employee is rare. Initially they have to be trained, but if they do the work, then they get the pay. If a task is not performed correctly, I first look to myself to make sure I have trained them properly."

"Would you blame any of your employees for not doing their job if for some reason they didn't get their pay?"

"Not at all, I would expect them not to work."

"Good. Now, we can create the same cause and effect accountability in your home environment that you create in your work environment. If it works in the adult world, why shouldn't it work at home?"

"But what if Don follows through on his threat of running away?" Mom was worried.

"How many of your employees have run away?"

She laughed.

I suggested that we create the same causes and effects in her home that she had so successfully created in her business. After all, Don will be spending more time in her kind of business world as an adult with greater need to succeed. Why not implement this same plan right now?

The philosophy behind the plan was simple: When you do something, you automatically receive a natural consequence for that action, good or bad. The only person that should really be concerned is the person who must live with the consequence. There is no screaming and yelling in the real world, and there should be no screaming and yelling at Don. There should, however, be a natural consequence for the action.

"Can we really do that with kids?"

"Absolutely," I said. "Not only does it work, but the kids love it."

"Great! But how?"

Since we were conferencing on the telephone, I told her to get a piece of notebook paper and draw a line down the middle. On one side I wanted her to write all the activities that Don likes to do on a daily basis. I suggested something to start her train of thought flowing. The list started to grow: riding his bike after school, riding his skateboard, watching television, going to the movies, having his friends spend the night, staying up later on weekend nights, and more. On the other side we listed all the activities that she would like him to do: cleaning his room, getting himself ready for school on time, completing all his homework, taking the garbage out, telling her whenever he's going out to play, setting the table for dinner, and more.

Up until now, Mom had merely expected Don to perform these duties with only whimsical, inconsistent rewards for his labors. If he wavered from his responsibilities, it was OK as long as it didn't bug her too much.

I laughed and said, "Is that the way you treat your employees?"

"No, we have a written contractual agreement."

"If it works so well at work, why shouldn't it work at home?" I asked. "Success is success. Your agreements at work require a certain amount of discipline from both you and your employee, but it also offers everyone involved complete freedom to concentrate on the important things in their life. Life is supposed to be fun. Sit down with Don, just like you do with your employees, and go over the list. Go over the contract. Tell him that he has certain things to do, one of which is cleaning up his room. Tell him if he cleans up his room, he'll be able to earn his daily privilege of watching television and playing with his skateboard, or whatever it is. Explain how that works just like at the place of employment: if they do their work, then they get their paychecks, and can enjoy their privileges of watching television, going out to dinner, or owning a nice home."

Don's mom understood, and within a week she reported that Don was cleaning his room, there were no more arguments, and he seemed to enjoy it. He also seemed to enjoy the privileges more than he did before. The law of cause and effect works again. Kids are just like adults in the business world, they have got to know that what they are doing is going to have an effect. Only then can they be in control of their wants. That's what everybody wants, to be able to have what they want. These daily actions will put them in a certain direction for a specific destination: Successful Adults.

I had a similar conversation with the father of 15 year old Erik who wasn't doing well in school: calls from teachers about misbehavior in the classroom, not completing school assignments, even not coming directly home from school. Dad was worried about the direction Erik's life seemed to be heading. He thought he had tried every punishment he could impose from restrictions to physical punishment, but with only minimal results. Every inch of progress was a struggle. Both father and son were unhappy and dissatisfied.

"Raising kids is the same as achieving at work," I said. "Are you happy in your job?"

"Yes I am," he answered. "And I'm looking forward to my bonus. My wife and I will be able to go on our vacation to Europe."

"What kind of performance bonus excites Erik?"

He didn't understand.

I had Erik's Dad make a list of all the things Erik looked forward to (Privileges). At the top of the list was his driver's license, a high priority for any youth. I suggested he sit down and explain to his son how bonuses and rewards are earned in the real world of work. I had him draw up a written contract stating that when Erik successfully completes a grading period, he can get his driver's license and keep it until the next grading period. Then it must be earned again. Now for the bonus: for every extra credit assignment Erik completes for any class, Dad puts ten dollars into a bank account for Erik's car.

Today Erik is driving his own automobile and has a high school diploma with a 2.0 average. He's not going to college, but he definitely knows how to succeed at a job.

Regardless if it's earning a paycheck or the privilege of riding a skateboard, each of us, including our kids, need to know we can control the consequences. If kids don't have that control, then everything just seems chaotic and pointless. In your eyes it doesn't appear that way because you know how the structure works. Kids don't know how the structure works; they need to be taught. That's your job as a parent and you do that by on-the-job training.

If you want to get it right, then you've got to write it down. To be successful takes a commitment, and making a commitment is making a written agreement.

Why something as formal as a written contract? Can't this just be a verbal agreement? Well, that's all a contract really is: a verbal agreement written down.

All relationships are contracts, an agreement between two people to act in a specific way for specific rewards. You may not always sit down and sign a piece of paper, but written or verbal they are contracts all the same.

Let's look at a rental contract as an example. A rental contract states required expectations while in a specific environment which allows the individual to remain in the environment. Perhaps such things as no pets, no smoking, being responsible for the garbage and outside maintenance, and rent due on the tenth of every month are written into the rental contract. If all these behaviors are followed, the tenant has the privilege of enjoying the house. If the tenant chooses not to meet the defined expectations, that's OK, but the tenant won't receive the privilege of being allowed to stay. This contract relationship happens between landlord and renter. Except for the monthly rent, it could be a contract between teenager and parent for use of the car.

If you are going to be using contracts in your home anyway, and we all do whether we are aware of them or not, design them for success. It's a lot easier and more fun if everyone knows exactly what they need to do in order to succeed.

To write our Contract, first take out your list of Expectations and look at them again. Revise them if necessary to include important details.

Now take out the list of Privileges and make sure it's complete.

The Contract should look like this:

Agreement between (Parent) and (Child).

If (Child) follows through on the following Expectations:

(Write them out)

Then (Child) gets to enjoy the following Privileges:

(Write them out)

(Child) understands that Privileges will only be given upon completion of

Expectations.

We have read and understand this agreement

(Signature of Child)   (Signature of Parent)   (Date)

The Contract merely connects the Privileges to the defined expectations, just like contracts do in the real world. A child's real job isn't to acquire the Privileges, it's to learn how to take responsibility for their actions, which will determine how many adult privileges they get to actually participate in. Who is in control? The kids are always in control, now, and consequently, they will be learning how to stay in control as an adult in the real working world.

What if the child has a specific behavior challenge that needs special attention now? Lets say the child refuses to complete any homework, or is constantly fighting at school, or is refusing to go to bed on time each and every night. Then you can sit down and write up a specific contract for that immediate behavior. When that behavior becomes part of the daily routine, after twenty-one days of keeping the contract, the special contract can gradually be faded away like a pair of crutches allowing the daily achievement of privileges and recognition to take control.

Can something so simple as a contract really change a behavior that has appeared to become so dominant? Kids don't want to be involved in unacceptable behavior. They really want to have the recognition like any other child, but for some reason the only way they've been able to achieve recognition is by involving themselves in the unacceptable behavior. The contract gradually changes the behavior of the child and the parents too. The parents can actually recognize what they have been doing to create that behavior, while they're learning how to get what they want.

But nothing happens overnight. Just as winning is not a game of chance but a purposeful effort, changing behavior is not a mystery or a miracle. Behavior changes gradually. Your child will have the good behavior on for a while and then bad again, just to keep The System honest. That's why the bad behavior occurs, just to test The System for its honesty and consistency. Do you remember when the speed laws went to 55 mph? Did everyone go 55 mph? They went to 55 mph for a while and then back to 65 mph to see if it was really going to be enforced, going back up and down depending on the consistency of the system. Then there was a group of truckers who really got upset and displayed outrageous behavior trying to eliminate the system.

If when the child exhibits bad behavior, you decide to give in just a little, thinking it wouldn't hurt, then the child has proven there is no system. There is no consistency and no control. The child's usual behavior continues but this time at probably a more erratic level than before. The parents are now surely convinced that the child is bad and The System doesn't work. But if the parents follow The System consistently through the behavioral flare-ups, the bad behavior will gradually disappear.

The contract takes care of all the details and the Behavior Rule of Thumb takes care of the decisions. It's just like the contract between landlord and renter. The contract handles everything, that is unless the landlord or the renter is allowed to deviate just once from the Expectations. Then there is only bickering, indecision, and heartache from not knowing what to do. When you know what to do and how to do it, the heartache disappears and you begin a happy, productive relationship with your successful children.

6

A Word of Encouragement

Be patient. You can only live one day at a time. You need only to succeed today to guarantee a successful future for your kids. Live successfully one day at a time. Don't try to do tomorrow's work today, just take it from morning until night. If you go to bed each night knowing that you performed your best, then you are raising your kids for success. Go to sleep with peace of mind because you know you're in control.

Remember to reward *yourself* each day, as well as your kids. Know that you've done your best for the day and schedule in something special like a relaxing cup of tea or a soothing bath. Look in the mirror each morning and evening and tell yourself "Great day. Each day just gets better and better."

You must reward yourself. Nobody else will. Without a reward for the effort, you eventually won't do the work because you're not getting the pay. The

System applies to you, too.

Remember the list of questions you answered about your children's behavior at the end of Chapter One? At the end of every thirty days, ask yourself these questions again. You'll be surprised at the progress. Progress is difficult to see on a day to day basis because raising kids for success is like building a brick building: you spend all of your time concentrating on the bricks and need to step back from time to time to admire your work.

*   Do you have moody children around the house?

*   You don't look forward to seeing your kids every day?

*   Do you feel you need a break from the kids?

*   Is "No!" becoming an important word in your vocabulary around the house?

*   Do you spend more time disciplining your kids rather than enjoying their company?

*   Does your kid's behavior get on your nerves, daily?

*   Do you find yourself nagging more than laughing?

* Do you find yourself saying, "I guess it's OK. They'll probably grow out of it."

*   Is the school telling you your child is just going through a phase?

*   Do you find yourself thinking of fantasy dream vacations that don't include your kids?

*   Do you wonder what to do when you see them doing something annoying or inappropriate?

*   Are the kids in your life beginning to demand things rather than earn them?

*   Are you dining and whining more than you're wining and dining lately?

*   Are you using words like "hyperactive" at home or school to justify annoying behaviors?

If the answers to these questions show sincere progress, schedule something special to reward the entire family: a movie, dinner, a Sunday outing. When the new, workable behaviors have become the accepted, automatic behaviors in your family, plan a big reward, such as a vacation or other fun activity. As I was completing the writing of this book, I came across a letter in Dear Abby that I would like to share with you:

DEAR ABBY: Your answer to "No Win Situation" rang a bell with me. "No Win" asked whether she should tell her friend/"Jane," that she was cutting down her visits to her (Jane's) house because of Jane's badly behaved children. You advised "No Win" that she should gently tell Jane as diplomatically as possible that her children's behavior is the problem. You pointed out that ill mannered and badly behaved children are obnoxious and therefore friendless.

Abby, I am the son of not one but two "Jane-type" parents. The result was just as you described. I grew up self-centered, ill mannered, badly behaved, obnoxious and friendless.

It all-worked out-finally. I am now 52 and fairly successful, but I struggled all my life with personality and attitude problems. My grade school report cards consistently showed low marks in "Respects the rights of others". I eventually learned how to be a human being. I was taught by the outside world. It would have been a lot easier had I learned those lessons at home.

COLONEL, USMC (RETIRED)

Every human being, every animal, every little baby, wants recognition. They want to be rewarded and they want to earn it. When they know how to be responsible for their actions to receive the love and rewards, we'll know we've raised our kids for success.

Bibliography

Berliner, David C, and N. L. Gage. *Educational Psychology.* Chicago: Rand McNally College Publishing Company, 1975, paperback.

Briggs, Dor thy Corkille. *Your Child's Self-Esteem: The Key to His Life.* New York: Doubleday & Co., Inc., 1970; Doubleday & Co., Inc., Dolphin Books, 1975, paperback.

Bristol, Claude. *The Magic of Believing.* New Jersey: Prentice-Hall, Inc.,

1957; New York: Cornerstone Library, Inc., 1967, paperback.

Buscaglia, Leo. *Living, Loving & Learning.* New York: Random House, 1982, paperback.

Carnegie, Dale. *How to Win Friends and Influence People.* New York: Simon & Schuster, Inc., 1936; Pocket Books, Inc., 1977, paperback.

Carnine, Douglas, and Jerry Silbert. *Direct Instruction Reading.* Columbus: Charles E. Merrill, 1979.

Dreikurs, Rudolf. *Psychology in the Classroom: A Manual for Teachers.* New York: Harper & Row, 1968.

Dreikurs, Rudolf, and Vicki Soltz. *Children: The Challenge.* New York: Hawthorn Books, 1964.

Dyer, Wayne. *The Sky's the Limit.* New York: Simon & Schuster, Inc., 1980.

Frankl, Viktor E. *Man's Search for Meaning.*

Revised edition, Boston: Beacon Press, Inc., 1963; New York: Pocket Books, Inc., 1975, paperback.

Gilmore, Susan K *The Counselor-In-Training.* New Jersey: Prentice-Hall, 1973.

Glasser, William, M. D. *Sdwols Without Failure.* New York: Harper & Row Publishers, Inc., 1969; Harper & Row Publishers, Inc., Perennial Library, 1975, paperback.

Hill, Napoleon. *Think and Grow Rich.* New York: Hawthorne Books, Inc., 1966: Fawcett World Library, 1976, paperback.

Hill, Napoleon, and W. Clement Stone. *Success Through a Positive Mental Attitude.* New York: Pocket Books, 1977, paperback.

Maltz, Maxwell, M. D. *Psycho'Cybemetics: The New Way to a Successful Life.* New Jersey: Prentice-Hall, Inc., 1960; Pocket Books, Inc., paperback.

Newman, James W. *Release Your Brakes.* New

York Warner Books, 1977, paperback. Nirenberg, Jesse S. *Getting Through to People.* New

Jersey: Prentice-Hall, Inc., 1963, paperback. Riesman, David. *The Formation of Character.* New

York: Holt, Rinehart and Winston, Inc., 1967. Ringer, Robert J. *Looking Out For #1.* New York:

Fawcett Crest Books, 1977, paperback. Sanford, John, and Paula Sanford. *The*

Transformation of the Inner Man: The

Complete Book on Inner Healing Today. Tulsa

OK: Victory House, Inc., 1982, paperback. Schmuck, Richard A. and Patricia A. Schmuck.

Group Processes in the Classroom. Iowa:

William C. Brown, 1979. Schuller, Robert H. *The Peak to Peak Principle.*

New York: Doubleday & Co., 1980. Schwartz, David J. *The Magic of Self Direction.* New

York: Simon & Schuster, Inc., 1965, paperback. Sloane, Howard N., et al. *Structured Teaching: A*

Design for Classroon Management and

Instruction. Illinois: Research Press Company,

1979. Sulzer, Beth, and G. Roy Mayer. *Behavior*

Modification Procedures for School Personnel.

New York: Holt, Reinhart and Winston, 1972. Waitley, Denis. *The Winner's Edge: The Critical*

Attitude of Success. New York: Times Books,

1980.

Wilson, James Q. "Raising Kids." *The Atlantic,*

October 1983, p. 45. Ziglar, Zig, *See You At the Top.* Gretna: Pelican

Publishing Co., 1980.